Oz Clarke's
Wine Buying
Guide 2006

**the essential companion to
Oz Clarke's Pocket Wine Book 2006**

D0709852

TIME WARNER
BOOKS
WEBSTERS

A TIME WARNER/WEBSTERS BOOK

This edition first published in 2005 by
Time Warner Book Group UK
Brettenham House
Lancaster Place
LONDON WC2E 7EN
www.twbg.co.uk

Created and designed by
Websters International Publishers Limited
Axe and Bottle Court
70 Newcomen Street
LONDON SE1 1YT
www.websters.co.uk
www.ozclarke.com

Oz Clarke's Wine Buying Guide 2006 edition
Copyright © 2005 Websters International Publishers
Text copyright © 1992–2005 Oz Clarke

A CIP catalogue for this book is available from the British Library

ISBN 0-316-73058-0

Printed and bound by Mondadori, Verona, Italy

The information and prices contained in the Guide were correct to the best
of our knowledge when we went to press.
Although every care has been taken in the preparation of the Guide, neither
the publishers nor the editors can accept any liability for any consequences
arising from the use of information contained herein.
Oz Clarke's Wine Buying Guide is an annual publication. We welcome any
suggestions you might have for the next edition.

Editor Maggie Ramsay
Art Director Nigel O'Gorman
Editorial Assistant Ruma Islam
DTP Keith Bambury
Production Sara Granger, Emily Toogood
Managing Editor Anne Lawrance

Cover photograph Nigel James
Cover painting David Dean

CORPORATE SALES
Companies, institutions and other organizations wishing to make
bulk purchases of this or any other Oz Clarke title published by
Time Warner Books UK should contact Special Sales on
+44 (0)20-7911 8117.

ADVERTISING SALES
Tim Bradshaw
112 Highfield Lane
Hemel Hempstead
HERTS HP2 5JG
tel/fax 01442 231131

Contents

Introduction

I've got great news for you. There's a global surplus of wine this year that totals 7 billion, 600 million bottles. Yippee. Crack open the bubbly. English, of course.

I've got terrible news for you. There's a global surplus of wine this year that totals 7 billion, 600 million bottles. It's a catastrophe.

But it's the same news. Sure it is. And if British wine drinkers increase their annual consumption by 190 bottles each we could probably mop it up, but since we're each only getting through about 33 bottles annually at the moment, it'll demand a bit of a lifestyle change.

Well, this chitter-chatter is all very well. But what's the real situation in our world of wine? Is it healthy or are we heading for a bust? Are producers in a good or a bad way; are retailers gouging us for profit or are they our best buddies; are we wine drinkers having the time of our lives or are we being taken for a massive ride?

> 'Brands...pretend to come from somewhere, to be made by some-body special'

GLUT FEELING

Let's look at this glut business. How can you have such an imbalance between production and consumption? In any other sort of business, it simply wouldn't be allowed. Yet in wine we now have a surplus that is the worst in history, and will get considerably more serious over the next few years unless frost and hail, tempest and earthquake devastate the world's vineyards on an annual basis. Which is as unlikely as UK drinkers managing to increase their consumption overnight by almost 600% – that's what would be needed to balance supply and demand. If the entire French harvest were destroyed that might balance the books for a year. (Remember, France is the world's biggest producer with well over 20% of the global total.)

Or if the USA, Australia, Argentina and South Africa didn't pick a grape this year, that might briefly tilt things back into balance.

But then it might not, because many of the vineyards in the New World are so new they've either produced no crop at all yet, or only a limited one. And it's not just the New World. Spain has replaced 40,000 hectares of vineyards since 2001 and they are so far only producing at 30% capacity. Add to this the fact that the area under vine is still increasing in such serious New World wine countries as Argentina, Chile, South Africa and New Zealand and that surplus doesn't exactly look as though it will fall next year.

And Australia? Between 1996 and 2002 Australia doubled its wine production. In 2004 it had its biggest ever harvest, until 2005 came along which was even bigger. And being Australia, they busted a gut to try to export what they'd made. Exports rose by 148 million bottles in 2004–2005. Not enough. The surplus boomed to 260 million bottles of Aussie grog. Who's going to drink it? In the UK we drank more than 30 million extra bottles of wine last year. You'd need eight thirsty United Kingdoms to clear just the *Aussie* surplus.

And don't talk to me about China. The fastest-growing vineyard area in the world is in China. It's increased by more than 100,000 hectares since 2000 and already matches the USA. Despite efforts to make the Chinese a wine-drinking nation, there are no signs of it happening yet – in a two-and-a-half week trip to the Chinese hinterland this year, I did not see one single Chinese person drink wine. Are they going to tip all their wine into the gutter? Or are they going to try to sell it abroad? And who'll buy it? Us?

ON THE SHELF? AT A PRICE

It would be nice to say – hey, isn't this glut a laugh, loads of cheap booze for everyone. But the world doesn't work like that. Take our market. The areas with the biggest surplus to shift are European – especially French. They've got loads of wine and they'll listen to any half-sensible offer. But what if the offer from a British supermarket buyer is prefaced by – of course, I'll need £50,000 as a listing fee for your wine. You think I'm joking? Increasingly that's the kind of money you have to pay to get listed, to get your wines on a gondola end, to get on the shelf at eye level. If you're on the gondola end, supermarkets reckon you increase your sales 22 times! So pay up for the privilege. Oh, and fund a discounting spree. You think your wine should sell at £6.99? Be prepared to sell most of it at £4.99 or less. Now, many smaller estates hardly turn over £50,000, let alone make that sort of profit. Margins are tight in the world of wine production. That's the world of good wine production, fairly priced wine production.

But there is one area where the margins are at the very least flexible. The Big Brands. They have enormous marketing budgets, and our supermarkets and High Street retailers know this. The Big Brands can not only pay listing fees, but they can fund discounting. They don't like it, because it cuts into their profits, but they have a flexibility that a small producer cannot afford. They hike the normal selling price so that when it's slashed back by 30, 40 or 50% it looks like a fantastic bargain to us consumers, but the *real* reduction from what it's actually worth is often minimal. And because it's a brand, they can reduce the quality of the wine in the bottle. The general rule is – buy cheaper wine but blend in more sugar, because sugar masks the nastiness of the raw materials, just as it does in a poor cup of tea. And they think no one will notice.

This doesn't make Brands sound very attractive. Well, frankly, most of them aren't. They're not in the 'giving pleasure to the consumer' game – however much they trill on about how their products *must* be good because lots of people buy them. If millions hadn't been spent on promoting them, *no one* would buy them. They pretend to come from somewhere in particular, to be made by somebody special, but in truth they come from nowhere and are made by nobody in particular. Do you really think there is a Monsieur J P Chenet? Is Rosemount Estate really from an estate? Do Gallo really grow their California grapes in a place with the unlikely name of 'Sierra Valley'?

REAL PEOPLE, REAL PLACES, REAL WINE

And yet it is 'brands' that are held out as the saviours of producers in this period of glut. France has a major glut problem. She has never produced more wines of quality and personality than she does now, yet it seems we won't buy them. The reason given is that they are too difficult to understand, so the French are told they should adopt 'New World'-style branding. The great strength of France – and many other European countries – is their sense of 'somewhereness'. Must we lose this to cope with the global glut? I'd much rather rip up the vines that aren't good enough, and I'd much rather expend as much effort and enthusiasm as I can muster on asking all of you to buy wines with a sense of somewhere and somebody. This has always been at the heart of good wine – and it still is. Look at the winners of our tastings this year. New World or Old, it's people and a sense of place that count. If we all decide that these are the wines *we* want, we can begin to push back the tide of gutless 'branded' wines that are threatening to swamp our fascinating and precious world of wine.

Wine finder

RED WINES
VdP = Vin de Pays

Under £5
Badgers Creek 80
Bonarda-Sangiovese, Santa Julia, Familia Zuccardi 92
Brindisi Rosso, Cellino San Marco 75
Cabernet Franc, Touraine 44
Cabernet Sauvignon, First Flight 77
Cabernet Sauvignon-Shiraz, Lost Sheep, Evans & Tate 76
Cabernet Sauvignon-Carmenère, Old Vines, Doña Dominga, Casa Silva 74
Carmenère, Cielo de Luz 79
Carmenère, Los Robles 44
Chenin Blanc, Peter Lehmann 48
Chianti, Casa Laora 78
Chilean Red, Santa Clara, Viña Requinga 51
Claret (Morrisons) 80
Garnacha, Vineyard X, Bodegas Borsao 50, 92
Garnacha-Tempranillo, La Riada 46
Hearty Red (Asda) 78
Merlot, Chilean (Sainsbury's) 79
Merlot, Chilean, Santa Lucia 80
Merlot Reserve, Chilean (Tesco) 74
Merlot-Malbec-Cabernet Sauvignon, Dancing Monkey 48
Mighty Murray Red, Andrew Peace 50
Minervois, Ch. Villerambert-Moreau 49
Montepulciano d'Abruzzo, Collezione Italiana 80
Nero d'Avola, Inycon 48
Petite Sirah, The Boulders 75
Pinot Noir, Cono Sur 46
Pinot Noir, Morandé 76
Portuguese Red (Sainsbury's) 81
Primitivo-Merlot, Da Luca 46
Rioja, Viña Caña 76
Rioja, Bodegas Navajas 79
Ruby Cabernet-Shiraz, Australian 80
Saint Roche, VdP du Gard, Dom. de Tavernel 77
Sangiovese, Argentine, La Agricola 78
Shiraz, Chilean (Sainsbury's) 77
Shiraz, Crow's Landing 51
Shiraz, El Dueño, Bodegas Esmeralda 76
Shiraz, First Flight Reserve 76
Shiraz, Palandri 74
Shiraz, Wildcard, Peter Lehmann 44
Shiraz-Cabernet Sauvignon, First Flight 77
Syrah, Oak-aged, Trivento, Concha y Toro 73
Syrah, VdP d'Oc, Herrick 48
Tempranillo, Dragon, Berberana 51
Tempranillo-Merlot, Altozano 51
Zinfandel, Californian Reserve, Jeff Runquist 75

£5–£10
Almansa, Marqués de Rojas, Bodegas Piqueras 42
Beaujolais, J-F Garlon 40, 92
Blaufränkisch, Erwin Tinhof 43
Bonarda, Alamos 39
Bourgueil, La Coudraye, Yannick Amirault 92
Brindisi Rosso, Cantine Due Palme 95
Cabernet Sauvignon, Chapel Hill 61, 94
Cabernet Sauvignon, Errázuriz 42
Cabernet Sauvignon, Founder's Block, Katnook 36
Cabernet Sauvignon, Kangarilla Road 32
Cabernet Sauvignon, Nativa, Carmen 61, 94
Cabernet Sauvignon, Peñalolén 39
Cabernet Sauvignon Reservado, Anakena 71
Cabernet Sauvignon Reserve (Co-op) 70
Cabernet Sauvignon Reserve, Haras de Pirque 22
Cabernet Sauvignon, Ruca Malen 34
Cabernet Sauvignon, Springfield Estate 94
Cabernet Sauvignon, Winemaker's Selection, Veramonte 40
Cabernet Sauvignon, Wrattonbully Vineyard, Evans & Tate 64
Cabernet Sauvignon-Malbec, Catena Zapata 68
Carignan Vieilles Vignes, VdP de Caux, Dom. de Nizas 21
Carmenère, Gracia de Chile Reserva 72
Châteauneuf-du-Pape, Les Vignerons des Dentelles Vaucluse 72
Côtes de Castillon, Seigneurs d'Aiguilhe, Ch. d'Aiguilhe 66
Côtes du Rhône-Villages Sablet, Dom. le Souverain 38
Côtes du Roussillon-Villages Tautavel, Le Mascarou, Dom. des Chênes 39
Côtes du Ventoux, Fayard, Dom. de Fondrèche 38
Dolcetto d'Alba, Magna, Paolo Manzone 34
Douro, Valtorto 48
The Fergus, Tim Adams 31
Grenache, Peter Lehmann 22
Grenache-Shiraz, 'DNA', Tim Smith Wines 21
Lacrima di Morro d'Alba, Rubico, Marotti Campi 94
Mâcon-La-Roche-Vineuse, Alain Normand 37
Malbec, Ricardo Santos 33
Malbec Reserve, Lizards of Oz 68
Merloblu, Castello di Luzzano 43
Merlot-Carmenère-Cabernet, Trio, Concha y Toro 67
Minervois, Cuvée Prestige, Ch. du Donjon 22
Nero d'Avola-Syrah, Benuara, Cusumano 95
Parcela #7 Reserva, Viña von Siebenthal 36
Petite Sirah, L A Cetto 95
Pinot Noir, De Loach 42

7

Wine finder

Sauvignon Blanc, Oracle 49
Sauvignon Blanc, Riverview 51
Sauvignon Blanc, Viño Ulmo 78
Semillon-Chardonnay, Santa Lucia 81
Semillon-Sauvignon Blanc, Palandri 44
Soave Classico, Zenato 74
Viña Sol, Torres 96
Viognier, The Boulders 48
Viognier, Cono Sur 44
Viognier, VdP d'Hauterive, Dom. de la Bastide 46, 98

£5–£10

Alsace, Terroirs des Châteaux Forts, Rolly Gassmann 20
Bourgogne Hautes Côtes de Nuits, Dom. Thevenot-Le Brun 18
Chablis, Cave des Vignerons de Chablis 70
Chardonnay, Chalker's Crossing 33
Chardonnay, The Olive Grove, D'Arenberg 98
Chardonnay, Rustenberg 67
Chardonnay, The Society's Australian 42
Chardonnay, Unoaked, Errázuriz 43
Chardonnay, Warwick Estate 98
Chardonnay, Winemaker's Lot, Concha y Toro 97
Chardonnay-Viognier-Marsanne, Novas 98
Chenin Blanc, Peter Lehmann 96
Gewurztraminer, Francis Klee 72
Gewurztraminer, Kuehn 98
Gewurztraminer, Villa Maria Private Bin 99
Gewurztraminer, Winemaker's Lot, Concha y Toro 99
Grenache-Viognier, La Croix Belle, VdP des Côtes de Thongue 38
Grüner Veltliner, Moosburgerin, Weingut Felsner 68
Ktima Papagiannakos 96
Lugana, Villa Flora, Zenato 96
Mâcon-Chardonnay, White Burgundy, Cuvée Paul Talmard 38, 97

Minervois Blanc, Cuvée Inés, Le Moulin des Nonnes 31
Moschofilero, Tselepos 31
Pinot d'Alsace, Beblenheim, Dom. Bott-Geyl 35
Riesling, Tim Adams 97
Riesling, Brown Bros 38
Riesling Spätlese, von Hövel, Scharzhofberg 66
Rioja Malvasia, Martin Cendoya 35
Rioja (barrel fermented), Torresoto, CVNE 66
Sauvignon Blanc, Clifford Bay 24
Sauvignon Blanc, Clocktower, Wither Hills 66
Sauvignon Blanc, Floresta, Santa Rita 62
Sauvignon Blanc, Garuma Vineyard, Viña Leyda 16
Sauvignon Blanc, Jackson Estate 97
Sauvignon Blanc, Life from Stone, Springfield Estate 97
Sauvignon Blanc Reserve, Montes 42
Sauvignon Blanc, Tamar Ridge 32
Sauvignon Blanc, Waipara West 19
Sauvignon Blanc-Semillon, Sainsbury's Classic Selection, Capel Vale 71
Semillon, Tim Adams 12
Semillon, Estate Reserve, Denman Vineyards 70
Semillon, Peter Lehmann 98
Semillon, Steenberg 98
Torrontes, Crios de Susana Balbo, Dominio del Plata 40, 98
Valdeorras Godello, Gabo do Xil, Telmo Rodríguez 36
Verdelho, Chapel Hill 33
Vinho Verde, Quinta de Simaens 97
Viognier Grande Réserve, VdP d'Oc, Dom. Cazal Viel 37

Over £10

Bourgogne Blanc, Dom. de Montmeix 97
Chardonnay, Diamond Valley Vineyards 13
Chardonnay, Moonambel, Dalwhinnie 12
Meursault (Tesco) 67

Sauvignon Blanc, Ashbrook Estate 19
Sauvignon Blanc-Semillon, Cape Mentelle 97
Sauvignon Blanc-Semillon, Suckfizzle 18
Savennières, L'Enclos, Eric Morgat 25
Vieilles Vignes, VdP des Pyrénées-Orientales, Dom. le Roc des Anges 25
Zind, Zind-Humbrecht 64

INDEX OF PRODUCERS

Wine finder

Top 20

This is an inspiring bunch of wines, bursting with personality and humming with the kind of excitement that entices wine drinkers deep into the spider's web of wine, turning them from mere consumers into devoted wine lovers, unable to resist the lure of the new, the original, the passionate. This is where the heart of wine beats strong, with memorable flavours created by unforgettable people in beautiful places that etch themselves into your consciousness. And though most of them are sold by independent wine merchants, there are wines in here from Tesco, Waitrose, Oddbins and Majestic. Anyone, big or small, *can* sell great wine. They just have to decide that they *will*, and that the route to survival and prosperity is to seek out consumers who care, rather than piling the wines high, selling them cheap.

❶ 2001 Cabernet Sauvignon, Domus Aurea, Maipo Valley, Chile, £16.99, Oddbins

Domus Aurea is from the Quebrada de Macul vineyard, perched high above the city of Santiago, tucked into the slopes of the Andes Cordillera. In fact it's closer to the Andes than any other Chilean vineyard, and it's so cool that they only *start* picking when everyone else is just finishing their vintage party. But the sun shines through the cool air and ever so slowly ripens the grapes. The result of this cool, long ripening is fabulous flavour and fabulous texture. But for wine this good you also need a passionate winemaker – and this wonderful Cabernet was made by the original genius of modern Chilean wine, Ignacio Recabarren. There are many excellent young winemakers now in Chile, but Ignacio blazed the trail, drawing out purity of fruit, intensity of perfume and a true sense of place in Chilean wines. And what does it taste like? Well, this wine has an intensity of blackcurrant fruit you may never have experienced before, a fabulous lush softness of texture which rides easily alongside some very noticeable but marvellously mellow tannins. And coiling through this, like strands of mist through a lowland forest, are exquisite herbal scents of eucalyptus and mint and sage. These flavours come from the place, and from the man.

Please bear in mind that wine is not made in infinite quantities – some of these may well sell out, but the following year's vintage should then become available.

❷ **2003 Shiraz, Heartland, Directors' Cut, Limestone Coast/
Langhorne Creek, South Australia, £12.99, Great Western Wine**
Talking of a sense of place and a passionate winemaker –
here's another beauty. This comes from the Wirrega Vineyard
in Australia's Limestone Coast, a great swathe of land covering

the bottom end of South Australia.
Wirrega is one magic patch of land in
the middle of nowhere (I know how to
get there. You turn right at a place called
Keith, drive for 50 km into the bush, turn
left, drive even further into the bush,
turn left again – haven't seen a soul for
an hour – it really is like that). But the
fruit for these wines is superb. Add a
brilliant young winemaker, Ben Glaetzer, and you get one of
the densest, yet most magical Shirazes in all Australia – a
fabulous mix of black plum and blackcurrant, rolled in black
chocolate, stirred in with beef tea and licorice and rubbed
with the zest of a superripe lime and the oil dripping from the
leaves of a eucalyptus tree. Irresistible texture. Irresistible
flavour. Irresistible sense of place. *Also at Nidderdale, Oz Wines.*

❸ **2002 The Aberfeldy, Tim Adams, Clare Valley, South
Australia, £18.99, Australian Wine Club**
Here, we've got a vineyard of ancient Shiraz, planted in 1904 and

still bursting with vitality. And we've got the
supreme interpreter of Clare Valley fruit – Tim
Adams. Unlike many of the modern Barossa
beasts, which are so overblown you can hardly
drink them, this tastes invigorating, refreshing
and memorable – just what great wine truly is.
This isn't a 'created' icon wine. This vineyard has
been proving itself for a century, and Tim Adams
has been patiently learning its secrets ever since
he first tasted the tiny berries hanging on the
vine nearly 20 years ago. It's a heady mix of
blackberry, blackcurrant and black plum fruit,
leather and licorice, mocha coffee and toffee
cream and, soaring above it all, the smells of the wide open
spaces – eucalyptus and mint and lovage leaves.

❹ **2004 Semillon, Tim Adams, Clare Valley, South Australia,
£8.99, Australian Wine Club**
It's that man again. And once again he shows that a sense of
place is fundamental to his being. Look on the back label,
which proudly names the families who own the Semillon

For more wine recommendations see Oz Clarke's Wine Style Guide, pages 92–101

vines – his neighbours the Crawleys and
the Smyths, and the Adams family itself.
Those other families should be grateful to
Tim Adams, because before he decided it
could be the Clare's finest white, Semillon
grapes were blended away without a
trace. That's difficult to believe when you
taste this superb example. It starts out
with all the freshness of an apple orchard
and all kinds of apple flavours: fresh-
picked Cox's, fresh-pressed russet apple
juice, Bramleys made into jelly with just a
dab of blackberry. Even the acidity has the
sweet yet sharp core of a baked apple. And way in the
background presides a cool but sensuous cloud of creamy,
brazil nut oak. *Also at Tesco.*

**❺ 2002 Pinot Noir, Carrick, Cairnmuir Road Winery,
Central Otago, New Zealand, £19.95, Great Western Wine**
The word's out that the new Pinot Noir paradise may lie in a
few parched acres huddled beneath the snowfields of the far
south of New Zealand's South Island. A ski resort in winter,
yet a virtual desert in summer, this is *extreme* vineyard
terrain, and it proudly produces extreme wines. This is a
marvellous example. The colour is dark, the smell is of
chocolate and cherry and strawberry, promising lushness on
a grand scale. Well, the lushness is there – great texture,
black cherry, strawberry and chocolate – but where did that
scent of mint and lemon blossom come from? Wow, that's
some acidity, and it scrapes your tongue with the exotic
attack of lime zest. And yet it's still lush. Unlike any other
Pinot Noirs. Central Otago beckons.

**❻ 2003 Chardonnay, Diamond Valley Vineyards,
Yarra Valley, Victoria, Australia, £10.99, Oz Wines**
Delicacy, perfect balance, elegance, class – these are not words
that are applied that frequently to Aussie Chardonnays, but
Diamond Valley deserves all these descriptions. This is quite
simply the most delightful,
harmonious Chardonnay you could
find in either hemisphere. There's a
crystal clear morning sunlight
quality to the mellow peach, green
fig and pineapple fruit, the clove
and cinnamon is delicately
sprinkled across the surface of the
wine, and the texture suckles and
caresses your tongue.

Best buys

❼ 2001 Vacqueyras, Domaine le Clos de Caveau,
Rhône Valley, France, £10.75, Adnams

The southern Rhône has been pumping out more and more exciting wines in the past few years, and we can at last begin to judge just how good these hillside villages can be. Vacqueyras can be very good indeed. It's tucked in close to

both Gigondas and Châteauneuf-du-Pape, but is less fleshy than these two wines: you almost feel that the sun-drenched grape juice was run over a bed of stones on the way to becoming wine. Soused with herbs too, in an attempt to stop the fabulous fruit seeming too come-hither and

beguiling. So we get a memorable fruit intensity of mulberry and ripe cherries, but it's as though their sweet syrup has congealed in the bottom of a baking dish. As though they tried to beat back the rocky tannins, the heady herbal scent and the arrogant rasp of ancient river stones, and then thought – no, age will soften them, we can wait.

---

❽ 2003 Shiraz, Tim Smith Wines, Barossa Valley,
South Australia, £15.99, Oz Wines

Whoever Tim Smith is, he's wasted no time in getting right to the heart of the Barossa, with this sincere and passionate expression of his old Shiraz vines near Tanunda. Rich deep,

serious wine – hey, hang on. Not *too* serious. Seriously irresistible perhaps, because the fruit here is so autumn-ripe it reminds me of plums left too late for picking as they leak syrup though their skins and wasps mob the bough. The fruit *is* treacly – black

treacle, syrup of figs and plums treacle – the chocolate is dark but not black, and someone's skimmed off the burnt top from a rice pudding – and yet it's all in balance. A Barossa classic.

---

❾ 2003 Lacrima di Morro d'Alba, Stefano Mancinelli,
Marche, Italy, £13.50, Bat & Bottle

The first time I tasted this wine was in the kitchen of the Italian wine expert Burton Anderson. He'd written that the flavour was so unusual he couldn't believe the stuff was actually made from wine grapes. I loved the wine then, and I love it now. Why? Exactly because it does taste *so* different. For a start, there is no more scented red wine. Open this bottle and the room is showered with the scent of rose petal, Fry's Turkish Delight, perfumed leather and the kind of sandalwood lotion a gentleman in a St James's club might allow his valet to pat on his cheeks. The taste in your mouth is full and ripe, the texture is good and there's even a little tannin. But none of this gets in the way of the riot of rose petal, sandalwood and scented talc jollity that makes the wine such fun.

---

⑩ 2002 Shiraz, Klauber Block, Kies Family Wines,
🍷 Barossa Valley, South Australia, £9.99,
Nidderdale Fine Wines

You usually have to pay twice as much to get such a blast of the Barossa Experience. And this wine *is* a palate blaster, gorgeously unsubtle, but the wallop of flavour stops you in your tracks and brooks no criticism from any red-blooded wine lover. It's as big and black as a chocolate soup, as dense as a stew of prunes and plums and blackberries and as lush as melted Harrogate toffee and cream caramels. Rich. Self-confident. Excellent.

⑪ 2003 Costières de Nîmes, La Bolida, Château d'Or et de Gueules, Rhône Valley, France, £19.30, Gauntley's

Costières de Nîmes is right at the bottom of the Rhône Valley,

where the hillsides disappear and the ancient riverbed fans out and slips exhaustedly towards the sea. But it deserves Rhône status, because the rich quality of the fruit is easily good enough, and the Nîmes perfume is exceptional for what are pretty warm conditions. This might almost seem too rich and stewy to start with – 2003 was a torrid year – but leave the bottle open half an hour and the seemingly overripe fruit reverts to a dense, syrupy lushness with a delightful and unexpected scent of sweet violets, while your palate appreciates the stony dryness that lingers in the aftertaste.

⑫ 2002 Merlot, Cuvée Alexandre, Casa Lapostolle, Colchagua Valley, Chile, £12.99, Booths

This is one of Chile's flagship wines and an excellent example of

international co-operation benefiting everybody. French and Chilean money and the crucial input of superstar French consultant Michel Rolland have produced a classic, dense red packed with dark chocolate and black plum richness but delightfully seasoned with the soy sauce savouriness and lily stem scent of Chile's thrilling Carmenère grape. It's powerful and burly now. But age it for 5–10 years and you'll confound any Old World fogies who say such New World wines won't develop. *Also available at L'Assemblage, Harvey Nichols, Laytons, Majestic, Portland Wine, Sainsbury's, Villeneuve Wines.*

⑬ 2004 Sauvignon Blanc, Garuma Vineyard, Viña Leyda, Leyda Valley, Chile, £7.95, The Wine Society

This is in a silly, overweight bottle, but the wine inside is explosively good. It comes from the small new coastal area of Chile called Leyda: the flavours Leyda can achieve with Sauvignon Blanc are so thrilling it could outstrip Marlborough in New Zealand for quality – so long as it is not overhyped and over-exploited. This is a carnival parade of

mangetout peas, lime, capsicum, kiwi fruit, coffee bean and blackcurrant leaf. And the wine is 13.5% alcohol. It shouldn't be possible to get such green flavours and yet such alcoholic ripeness, but Leyda can do it.

Explore a new world

Chile - A great place to make wine

The long, thin country running down the west coast of South America - is blessed with perfect conditions for winemaking.

- Limarí Valley
- Aconcagua Valley
- Casablanca Valley
- San Antonio Valley
- Maipo Valley
- Cachapoal Valley ⎫ Rapel
- Colchagua Valley ⎰ Valley
- Curicó Valley
- Maule Valley
- Itata Valley
- Bío Bío Valley
- Malleco Valley

VALPARAISO

SANTIAGO

SAN ANTONIO

PICHILEMU • RANCAGUA

SANTA CRUZ • SAN FERNANDO

• CURICO
• MOLINA

• CONSTITUCION
• TALCA

SAN JAVIER •
• LINARES

• CAUQUENES

• CHILLAN

• CONCEPCION

The Andes Mountain Range

Border

WINES OF CHILE

www.winesofchile.org

⑭ 2003 Coteaux du Languedoc La Clape, La Falaise, Château de la Negly, Languedoc, France, £11.95, H & H Bancroft

Château de la Negly is a revitalized property in La Clape – one of the most potentially memorable areas in all of the

Languedoc – where virtually every one of the admittedly few single domaines makes wines of tremendous character. This is magnificent stuff – almost baked by the relentless 2003 sunshine, but still managing to come up with a bridesmaid's bouquet of violet scent, then apples peep through the lush, absurdly drinkable black cherry, black plum and licorice heart of the wine, occasionally fending off the brusque attentions of aromatic hillside herbs.

⑮ 2002 Sauvignon Blanc-Semillon, Suckfizzle, Augusta, Margaret River, Western Australia, £16, Great Northern Wines, Sommelier, Noel Young

Fascinating wine. This comes from vineyards absolutely at the bottom tip of the Margaret River region in Western Australia – considerably cooler than traditional Margaret River vineyards – and it's clearly a fantastic region for whites. This has tangy coffee bean and nettle and green syrup fruit, yet it's been made in oak, so it also has a softness of croissant and dry chocolate that makes for a truly classy white.

⑯ 2000 Rioja, Roda II, Spain, £19.99, Oddbins

Very much the shining new face of Rioja: red wines that are powerful, expressive – and expensive. If you think Roda II is expensive, well, there's a Roda I that will set you back

£29.99! (top stuff, though). If you like the gentle, creamy style of traditional Rioja (I do), you may find this a bit too much of a mouthful, but it's fine wine by any standard, with dense stewed plum and blackberry fruit, reasonable tannin and a lovely sheen of polished vanilla wood.

Everything's just a little more concentrated and intense than traditional Rioja.

⑰ 1999 Bourgogne Hautes Côtes de Nuits, Domaine Thevenot-Le Brun, Burgundy, France, £9.50, Irma Fingal-Rock

This is the kind of wine you go to an independent wine merchant for. A little-known producer in an obscure village miles from the glitzy world of Meursault and Puligny-

Montrachet, yet producing flavours to rival either – and at half the price or less. This wine is a triumph. It has all the coolness of the high hills where the vineyards are, but also the warm ripeness of the super 1999 vintage. The fruit is an austere, distant white apple

flesh, unadorned and lain on a rocky hillside; the weight and richness is oatmeal porridge and beeswax and a touch of bacon fat – and when you've swallowed the wine and you're smiling contentedly you realize there's something surprisingly pheromonic and sexy about the whole experience.

18 2004 Sauvignon Blanc, Ashbrook Estate, Margaret River, ♀ Western Australia, £10.95, Vin du Vin

Another bone-dry but flavour-packed snappy white wine to put New Zealand's Marlborough on its mettle. This has wonderfully pure green flavours, mouthwatering and aggressive yet ripe as well. That's the magic of Margaret River. Nettles and passion fruit, green capsicum and blackcurrant leaf, and a flavour like a green coffee bean all jostle and shout and demand attention, pleading to quench your thirst. And they will, if you let them.

19 2003 Clos de los Siete, Michel Rolland, Mendoza, ♂ Argentina, £10.99, Majestic Wine

This looks like becoming a role model for similar enterprises in Argentina. The vines are situated in some of Mendoza's higher vineyards, and the grapes clearly appreciate the conditions. This is splendid stuff – rich plum and prune fruit with a good herb rasp and grainy tannin that

adds bite to lovely chocolaty texture and sweet nutty oak.

20 2004 Sauvignon Blanc, Waipara West, ♀ Waipara, New Zealand, £8.99, Waterloo Wine Co

For those of us who really appreciate tangy, green-scented dry whites, here's a New Zealand example. Classic kiwi Sauvignon – with lashings of gooseberry, nettle, capsicum and lime fruit syrup and high acidity producing a wine that seems both rich and bone dry at the same time.

Runners-up

Another wonderful bunch of wines. Australia and France take the majority of the slots and show just how brilliant these countries can be when you move away from overhyped brands and overhyped wine regions.

❶ 2003 Shiraz, Tim Adams, Clare Valley, South Australia, £9.99, Australian Wine Club, Tesco

Tim Adams is probably Australia's most consistently excellent winemaker, producing just about every sort of red and white – and sweet, but not Chardonnay – in a style that sings triumphantly of the carefully husbanded Clare Valley vines. 2003 was a drought year down under just like it was here, but Adams coped and produced this sumptuous sweet-centred Shiraz. It's as rich as treacle tart coated with cocoa powder and melted milk chocolate but it's got a fruity core of Rosa plums and lime with a gentle scent of eucalyptus and mint.

❷ 2001 Shiraz, Bannockburn, Geelong, Victoria, Australia, £14.95, Lea and Sandeman

Bannockburn is one of Victoria's most famous wineries. Some of their wines are controversial, but they *do* make smashing Shiraz. It comes from cool vineyards in Geelong, south-west of Melbourne, and they give a quite different style of wine to warmer sites. And this is mature wine – 4½ years old and counting. It has a beautiful intensity of blackberry and loganberry fruit just touched by Rhône Valley smoke; it doesn't overpower, it gently persuades your palate; and the delectable cool yet subtly ripe flavour grows and grows in your mouth.

❸ 2003 Côtes du Roussillon-Villages, Cuvée Jean Julien, Domaine Seguela, Roussillon, France, £13.95, Mayfair Cellars

These are ferocious, sun-baked, wind-battered vineyards so far south in France you're almost in Spain. Until recently few people seemed to have worked out how to stop the relentless wind and sun from producing sullen reds, shorn of fruit and character. But a new generation is turning this baked backwater into a rising star for big reds. This is a dense, rich style, the superripe fruit almost crystallized, the plum and damson almost stewed to a treacle – but how did the fruit stay so fresh, and where did that violet perfume come from?

❹ 2002 Alsace, Terroirs des Châteaux Forts, Rolly Gassmann, France, £8.50, The Wine Society

Sometimes Alsace wines seem to be all fruit and orchard scent. But the name of this one tells you the soil is going to play a part. Certainly it is fruity – there's a haunting mix of white Williams pears and something that I described as 'old white peach syrup'. There's mellow honey, too, but like the hum of an electric cable, the taut mineral flavour of quartz dust never lets the fruit and honey out of its sight.

❺ 2003 Grenache-Shiraz, 'DNA', Tim Smith Wines, Barossa Valley, South Australia, £9.99, Oz Wines

Grenache and Shiraz is one of the great combinations – a real bacon and eggs, cheddar and chutney pairing, famous in France and equally famous in Australia. Grenache by itself is pure, high-octane happy juice. The Shiraz tries to add a breath of chocolate and coffee bean and plum but it's the Grenache that wins, with its fistfuls of hillside herbs, pepper that crackles on your tongue and gorgeous gluggable strawberry syrup.

❻ 2002 Zinfandel, Nepenthe, Adelaide Hills, South Australia, £19.99, Thresher

I don't know where Thresher found another cache of this: I thought we'd drunk it all last year. Well, it's back, a year older, and just as brilliant as before. A heady mix of dates and syrup of figs, rich brown fruits tumbled together with superripe blackberries and chocolaty plums, and through all this there is a tingling streak of sourness that intensifies the pleasure.

❼ 2003 Carignan Vieilles Vignes, Vin de Pays de Caux, Domaine de Nizas, Languedoc, France, £8.50, Mayfair Cellars

Ten years ago Carignan was derided as a junk grape, the curse of the Mediterranean. Now old-vines Carignan is being revered for what it is – a provider of absolutely smashing grog, the ultimate *drinking* red. And one that has thrilling texture – good acidity and tannin – as well as fascinating flavours of rich beef tea, dark stewed red cherries and a mineral streak as bright as glittering quartz.

❽ 2001 Cabernet Sauvignon-Merlot, Moda, Joseph, Primo Estate, South Australia, £18.99, Australian Wine Club

A wine which triumphantly proves that concentration and intensity *can* co-exist with finesse. Joe Grilli goes back to his Italian roots to make a wine in the style of the Amarones of the Veneto: Moda means *moda amarone*, or amarone-style. He dries his grapes in the sun before fermenting them, a process which imparts a black chocolate bitter edge – that's the *amarone*, or bitterness – but the true texture of the wine is thick and waxy, the fruit a sauce swimming in ripe damsons and loganberries and sweet melted chocolate, and someone dropped a swatch of leather in for extra perfume. Impressive now, this'll be a sensation at 15 years old.

Best buys

❾ 2002 Cabernet Sauvignon Reserve, Haras de Pirque, Maipo Valley, Chile, £7.50, Friarwood

Haras de Pirque has a reputation for making some of Chile's most serious Cabernets. It also has one of Chile's most spectacular wineries, horseshoe-shaped and cut into the mountainside – the owner is a successful racehorse breeder. This is impressive stuff, everything black and powerful: ripe blackcurrant and black plum fruit that's almost as rich as homemade jam, black treacle, bitter black chocolate. In short, a top Cabernet for now or up to 10 years.

❿ 2001 Shiraz Reserve, Belgravia, Orange, New South Wales, Australia, £10.50, Friarwood

This Shiraz comes from Orange, one of the highest and coolest vineyard regions in Australia – you can get snow in midsummer up here – and the result is marvellously intense, fragrant wines: the classic cool-climate combination. In this Shiraz, you can taste the cool, and it's a beautiful brow-soothing cool of gently ripe plum and loganberry, maybe blackberries too, wrapped round with a slightly sweet crusty bun toastiness and shot through with shards of chocolate.

⓫ 2002 Minervois, Cuvée Prestige, Château du Donjon, Languedoc, France, £7.95, Great Western Wine

The Languedoc – in which Minervois plays a leading role – is producing more fine wine now than at any time in its existence and this fairly priced wine is a good example. Lovely soft red, topped with cinnamon spice and bay leaf scent, stroked with leather perfume and filled out with rich, ripe strawberry fruit and a lush sweet red cherry core.

⓬ 2003 Grenache, Thiele Road, Schwarz Wine Company, Barossa Valley, South Australia, £16.17, Bordeaux Index

A pure, unashamed, unadulterated, exuberant expression of absurdly juicy, rich, overripe strawberry fruit. That's the taste. It's not complex or restrained. It's wonderfully rich and one-dimensional. Rich, syrupy, excellent. Not complex? Who cares?!

⓭ 2003 Grenache-Mataro-Shiraz, Tim Smith Wines, Barossa Valley, South Australia, £14.99, Oz Wines

The Mataro grape, a bit of a beast in the Barossa Valley if left unchecked, is what makes this wine harder, tougher, more reserved than the more usual Grenache-Shiraz blends. But leave the wine open an hour and a glorious transformation takes place. The bitterness dissolves into licorice and Harrogate toffee, strawberry fruit and crystallized plums assert themselves, and there's an invigorating medicinal seasoning of menthol and peppercorn.

BERKMANN
WINE CELLARS
— DIRECT —

FROM THE FINEST VINEYARDS
DIRECT TO YOUR DOOR

Award winning Berkmann Wine Cellars, suppliers to the
UK's top restaurants, bars and hotels, also offer a direct
to consumer service across the UK. Delivering prestige
wines from around the world direct to your door.

Italy

SPARKLING
Prosecco, La Marca (page 54)
Lambrusco, Medici Ermete (page 54)

WHITE
Fiano, Inycon (page 46)
Lugana, Zenato (page 96)
Soave Classico, Zenato (page 74)

ROSÉ
Rosato, Castello di Ama (page 96)

RED
Amarone della Valpolicella Classico, Vignale (pages 64, 95)
Brindisi Rosso, Cellino San Marco (page 75)
Brindisi Rosso, Due Palme (page 95)
Brunello di Montalcino, Casanova de Neri (page 95)
Chianti, Casa Laora (page 78)
Dolcetto d'Alba, Paolo Manzone (page 34)
Lacrima di Morro d'Alba, Stefano Mancinelli (page 14)
Lacrima di Morro d'Alba, Marotti Campi (page 94)
Merloblu, Castello di Luzzano (page 43)
Montepulciano d'Abruzzo (page 80)
Nero d'Avola, Inycon (page 48)
Nero d'Avola-Syrah, Cusumano (page 95)
Primitivo di Manduria, Pichierri Terrarossa (page 24)
Primitivo-Merlot, Da Luca (page 46)
Valpolicella Classico, Vigneti di Montegradella (page 73)

14 2004 Sauvignon Blanc, Clifford Bay, Marlborough, New Zealand, £9.95, Friarwood

Clifford Bay is a top new estate in the Awatere Valley, just south of the more famous Marlborough region. The vineyards sit on terraces right at the river mouth, the sunshine tempered by the sea breezes, and the fruit burnished to shining intensity. But it's a green intensity, not golden – everything green piles into the glass: nettles and capsicum, asparagus, and lime squeezed over passion fruit. There's a savoury scent of coffee beans too, and a rich texture that coats your mouth with all things green.

15 2003 Vin de Pays de la Principauté d'Orange, Terre de Bussière, Domaine de la Janasse, Rhône Valley, France, £7.49, Majestic Wine

Janasse is a super-fashionable Châteauneuf-du-Pape property making several levels of wine, and down at the bottom is this vin de pays. Bottom? This is fantastic stuff, it's just that the vineyards are outside the arbitrary line drawn by French lawmakers, so the wine sells for a quarter of the price. This wine is 14.5% alcohol, just like a top Châteauneuf, and is burly yet exotically rich, powerful and overripe. But it's a fabulous package of dense prunes and dates and sultanas, black chocolate ferocity and the hillside scent of lovage, sage and bay.

16 2002 Primitivo di Manduria, Pichierri Terrarossa, Savese, Puglia, Italy, £10.50, Bat & Bottle

We know the Primitivo grape better under its Californian name of Zinfandel. But as Primitivo, it was creating big, rich, ripe reds down in the heel of Italy long before it began slaking the thirst of goldminers in the Wild Wild West. The styles are similar in that they often have a cakey richness and a fat fudge and dates feel, but this Italian version adds a few turns of the black pepper grinder, some leather scent and just a splash of balsamic vinegar.

---

⑰ 2002 Savennières, L'Enclos, Eric Morgat, Loire Valley, France, £13.99, Raeburn Fine Wines

Savennières is *not* an easy wine to love. It's a haughty, aristocratic interpretation of the Chenin Blanc grape, in itself hardly a bobbydazzler. But I like this. I can feel the Chenin removing one or two of its layers and revealing a relatively charming disposition beneath. In fact the wine is positively honeyed, not in a syrupy, toast and butter way, but in a drier, sugarless way, as though the honey has been filtered through a bed of minerals. It tastes as though they threw flat, cold grey stones into the vat when the wine was fermenting. And the result is a joy.

---

⑱ 2001 Chardonnay, Moonambel, Dalwhinnie, Pyrenees, Victoria, Australia, £15.50, Playford Ros

It's not often we come across a mature Aussie Chardonnay (except under my stairs: there's loads of them there). Aussie Chardies have a reputation for not being able to age, but that reputation is based on fat, flabby, dumbed-down commercial blends from the hot areas of the country. Dalwhinnie is a quality-first producer in the cool-ish Victorian Pyrenees. And the result is a Burgundy-ish white of 4–5 years old with a toast and grilled cashew nuts smell, higher acidity than I expected (which will keep the wine young) and full, ripe, oatmeal and hazelnut flavours.

---

⑲ 2002 Navarra, Santa Cruz de Artazu, Spain, £15.95, James Nicholson

This is quite a lot of money for a Navarra red but it's certainly worth it. Rich, deep blackberry and loganberry fruit splashed with chocolate, but the fruit is appetizingly dry on your palate, powerful but not brutal, and balanced by the invigorating rasp of thyme and pepper and the cool grey sheen of slate.

---

⑳ 2003 Vin de Pays des Pyrénées-Orientales, Vieilles Vignes, Domaine le Roc des Anges, Roussillon, France, £11.69, Les Caves de Pyrene

Fascinating wine from the hot, windswept slopes inland from Perpignan almost on the Spanish border, that seems to exude a sense of place. There's a massive taste of stones and rocks, there's lanolin and pine resin, and is that orange peel I can taste? Try the wine – dense, brawny and rippling with personality – and decide for yourself.

Oz's top 20 clarets

Claret. It's another way of saying 'red wine from Bordeaux'. The £20,000 wines that occasionally make headlines are often red Bordeaux from historic vineyards, carefully matured in the cellar of a top restaurant for 20 years or more. At the other end of the spectrum are the 'everyday clarets' made to be drunk young, which can be found in high street shops for less than £10. In this section I've picked some clarets that may cost a little more, and will repay keeping for at least 5 years. These producers have, over the years, delivered consistently good wines, whether they come from the fabled gravels of Latour and Margaux, or from a largely unlauded pocket of magic dirt away from the bright lights. The wines below are listed in alphabetical order.

✪ **Château Batailley, Pauillac 2000 vintage is available from Berry Bros & Rudd for £28, or £22.40 if you buy 12 bottles**
Full, blackcurrant fruit overlaid with creamy vanilla and not too much tannin, Batailley shows fantastic consistency of flavour: I don't think there's been a bad vintage in the past quarter century. Lovely to drink at 5 years old, but will develop for at least 15 years.

✪ **Château Beau-Séjour Bécot, St-Émilion 2000 vintage is available from John Armit for £393.50 for 12 bottles**
On top form since the mid-1980s, Beau-Séjour Bécot is ripe, rich and firm-textured; it will need at least 8–10 years to develop.

✪ **Château Canon-la-Gaffelière, St-Émilion 2000 vintage is available from Farr Vintners for £600 for 12 bottles**
Owned by a German count, Stephan von Neipperg. His rich, concentrated but wonderfully balanced wines are at the top of the St-Émilion tree. They age over 10 years to a style which is powerful but serene.

✪ **Château Chasse-Spleen, Moulis 2001 vintage is available from Christopher Piper for £21.75, or £20.65 if you buy 12 bottles**
During the 1980s Chasse-Spleen built a reputation for ripe, concentrated and powerful wines; today these impressive wines easily reach Classed Growth standard every vintage, and start to peak at around 10 years old.

A NOTE ON PRICES
Prices are for one bottle, including duty and VAT but excluding delivery, unless otherwise stated. The vintages, retailers and prices are given as examples: the same wine may be available from a number of retailers, and either in bond or duty paid – prices vary widely. Some merchants only sell by the case; others offer a better price by the case than for a single bottle. Delivery charges may be negotiable depending on how much wine you buy. See also the retailers directory beginning on page 106. For further advice about buying Bordeaux for the long term see pages 102–105.

✪ **Château La Conseillante, Pomerol 2001 vintage is available from Corney & Barrow for £60.75**

If Pomerol's supposed to be a lush, seductive, scented style, La Conseillante does it superbly, year after year. Beautiful to drink at 5–6 years, but it can age much longer: I had a magnum of 1973 last year that was fading but divine.

✪ **Château Ducru-Beaucaillou, St-Julien 2001 vintage is available from O W Loeb for £48.47**

Traditionally the epitome of St-Julien, combining charm and austerity, fruit and firm tannins. Thrilling to drink, without ever being ostentatious. It is very enjoyable young, but much better after 20 years.

✪ **Château Ferrière, Margaux 2000 vintage is available from Nickolls & Perks for £364.54 for 12 bottles**

The wines are ripe, rich and perfumed, but above all have a wonderfully mellow, soothing texture.

✪ **Château Grand-Puy-Lacoste, Pauillac 1997 vintage is available from The Wine Society for £27, or £324 for 12 bottles**

Classic blackcurrant and cigar-box perfume. As the wine matures over 10 or even 20 years, the flavours mingle with the new oak sweetness and develop into one of Pauillac's most memorable taste sensations.

✪ **Château Haut-Bages Libéral, Pauillac 2001 vintage is available from Mayfair Cellars for £15.95**

The 1855 classification

This year is the 150th anniversary of the Bordeaux classification that determined which wines would have prestigious Cru Classé (Classed Growth) status. The 1855 list (below) included only red wines from the Haut-Médoc (and one from the Graves); the Graves and St-Émilion were classified later, while other areas of Bordeaux, such as Pomerol, have no *cru* system.

Premiers Crus/1st Growths Lafite-Rothschild; Margaux; Latour; Haut-Brion; Mouton-Rothschild.

Deuxièmes Crus/2nd Growths Rauzan-Ségla; Rauzan-Gassies; Léoville-Las-Cases; Léoville-Poyferré; Léoville-Barton; Durfort-Vivens; Gruaud-Larose; Lascombes; Brane-Cantenac; Pichon-Longueville Baron de Longueville; Pichon-Longueville Comtesse-de-Lalande; Ducru-Beaucaillou; Cos d'Estournel; Montrose.

Troisièmes Crus/3rd Growths Kirwan; d'Issan; Lagrange; Langoa-Barton; Giscours; Maléscot-St-Exupéry; Boyd-Cantenac; Cantenac-Brown; Palmer; La Lagune; Desmirail; Calon-Ségur; Ferrière; Marquis d'Alesme-Becker.

Quatrièmes Crus/4th Growths St-Pierre; Talbot; Branaire; Duhart-Milon; Pouget; La Tour-Carnet; Lafon-Rochet; Beychevelle; Prieuré-Lichine; Marquis de Terme.

Cinquièmes Crus/5th Growths Pontet-Canet; Batailley; Haut-Batailley; Grand-Puy-Lacoste; Grand-Puy-Ducasse; Lynch-Bages; Lynch-Moussas; Dauzac; d'Armailhac; du Tertre; Haut-Bages-Libéral; Pedesclaux; Belgrave; Camensac; Cos-Labory; Clerc-Milon; Croizet-Bages; Cantemerle.

Little-known property, whose lack of renown keeps the price just about reasonable. The style is positively hedonistic, with loads of delicious fruit, and the wines will age well.

✪ **Château Labégorce-Zédé, Margaux 1998 vintage is available from Seckford Wines for £170.96 for 12 bottles**
The wine isn't that perfumed, but is beautifully poised between concentration and finesse, and does have lovely black plum and black cherry fruit. Keep for at least 5 years before drinking.

✪ **Château Latour, Pauillac 2001 vintage is available from Jeroboams for £150**
Latour's renown is based on powerful, long-lasting classic wines. Its reputation for making fine wine in less successful vintages is well deserved, and in good vintages it soars. Latour's second wine, les Forts de Latour, is often a star performer.

✪ **Château Léoville-Barton, St-Julien 1999 vintage is available from Tanners for £36**
A traditionalist's delight. Dark, dry and tannic, and not overly oaked, over 10–15 years the wine reveals a lean yet magically balanced beauty rarely equalled in Bordeaux.

✪ **Château Lynch Bages, Pauillac 2001 vintage is available from Millésima for £450 for 12 bottles**
I am a great fan of Lynch-Bages, with its almost succulent richness, its gentle texture and its starburst of flavours, all butter, blackcurrants and mint. No longer underpriced, but it's worth the money. Impressive at 5 years, beautiful at 10 and irresistible at 20.

✪ **Château Malescot St-Exupéry, Margaux 2000 vintage is available from the Bordeaux Index for £405.48 for 12 bottles**
Once one of the most scented, exotic reds in Bordeaux. In the 1980s Malescot lost its reputation, but since 1995 it has begun to rediscover its cassis and violet perfume and has now returned to its former irresistible, perfumed, delicate glory.

✪ **Château Margaux, Margaux 2001 vintage is available from Friarwood for £161.50**
The most beautifully sculpted, the most fragrantly perfumed and the most consistently excellent of the great Médoc reds.

✪ **Château Pichon-Longueville, Pauillac 1995 vintage is available from Lay & Wheeler for £45.95**
Formerly known as Pichon-Baron, this property makes wines of rich, dark fruit and firm tannic structure, which need to be kept for at least 10 years, and will usually last for 30.

✪ **Château Pichon-Longueville-Lalande, Pauillac 1999 vintage is available from Peter Wylie Wines for £25**
Owned by May-Eliane de Lenquesaing, whose commitment and passion have made Pichon-Lalande one of the most prized wines of the Médoc. Divinely scented and lush at 6–7 years, the wines usually last for 20 at least.

✪ **Château Potensac, Médoc 2002 vintage is available from Averys for £14.94, or for £179 for 12 bottles**

Potensac's fabulous success is based on a dark, dense plum and cherry fruit, beautifully seasoned with oak – and a consistency without parallel. The wine can be drunk at 4–5 years, but fine vintages will improve for at least 15 years.

✪ **Château Siran, Margaux 2001 vintage is available from Portland Wine Co for £25**
Consistently fine wine: dark, soft, subtly scented. It's approachable young, but has enough structure to last for as long as 20 years.

✪ **Château Sociando-Mallet, Haut-Médoc 2000 vintage is available from Roberson for £52.95**
The wine shows every sign of great red Bordeaux flavours to come – if you can hang on for 10–15 years. In some vintages people think it's as good as a First Growth – and it is.

BUYING BORDEAUX WINE

The following merchants either specialize in fine Bordeaux wine or else regularly have an impressive selection of Bordeaux wines to choose from. Full details for these merchants can be found in our retailers directory, starting on page 106. Many other merchants listed in the retailers directory offer Bordeaux en primeur and pride themselves on tracking down parcels of high-quality claret only available in small quantities.

✪ Adnams, John Armit, L'Assemblage, Averys
✪ Berry Bros & Rudd, Bibendum, Bordeaux Index, Butlers
✪ Cave Cru Classé, ChâteauOnline, Corney & Barrow
✪ Direct Wine Shipments
✪ Farr Vintners, Fine & Rare Wines (www.frw.co.uk/ 020 8960 1995), Friarwood
✪ Goedhuis
✪ Jeroboams, S H Jones, Justerini & Brooks
✪ Lay & Wheeler, Lea & Sandeman, O W Loeb
✪ Mayfair Cellars, Millésima
✪ James Nicholson, Nickolls & Perks
✪ Christopher Piper, Playford Ros, Portland Wine
✪ Roberson
✪ Seckford Wines
✪ Tanners
✪ The Wine Society, Peter Wylie
✪ Noel Young Wines

£7 to £10

We had a very positive response to our new section, 'Under £7', last year, so we thought we'd go one better this year and have a £7–10 section as well. Stepping over the £6.99 price point allows everybody to spread their wings and offer wines of unbeatable personality and value for money. That's what the independent trade should stand for, and that's what they've demonstrated in this section.

❶ 2002 The Fergus, Tim Adams, Clare Valley, South Australia, £9.99, Australian Wine Club

You just can't keep this guy down; Tim Adams offers such stimulating, original wines, and here's another one. This is phenomenal stuff. I love the way Adams puts the family name of the vineyard owners on his label: here it's Mahon, Kelly and McDowell/Allen – thanks, folks, for persevering with Grenache when all around you people were grubbing it up. As for flavour, I know no wine like this one, none that dares to mix such unlikely bedfellows as lime zest, peppermint leaf and pungent eucalyptus with chocolate and strawberry syrup and a peppery rasp of tannin that is welcome to try to stiffen up the insane drinkability of this dangerous, irresistible, beautiful beast of a wine. *Also at Tesco.*

❷ 2003 Minervois Blanc, Cuvée Inés, Le Moulin des Nonnes, L & H Andrieu, Languedoc, France, £8.75, The Wright Wine Co

This is a rarity – and a delicious one – dry white wine from the red wine redoubt of Minervois in southern France. But there are patches of Minervois that are excellent for white wine, since the appellation clambers up the daunting slopes of the Montagne Noir to some considerable height. This is rich, round, exotic, but dry. Full of the autumnal flavours of dates and quince and medlars, the softness of Danish pastry and the perfume of toasted coriander seeds – and marvellously, intriguingly dry.

❸ 2003 Moschofilero, Tselepos, Mantinia, Greece, £7.25, The Wine Society

Here's a true original for white wine lovers who are beginning to tire of the mainstream world of Sauvignon and Chardonnay. It's very dry and, remarkably, smells and tastes of both the flower and the zest of citrus fruits – grapefruit, orange, lemon, but not lime – mixed with just a hint of grapiness and the palate-cleansing dryness of slate and stones.

For more wine recommendations see Oz Clarke's Wine Style Guide, pages 92–101

Aussie Shiraz

The Aberfeldy, Tim Adams (page 12)

Klauber Block, Kies (page 15)

Shiraz, Tim Adams (page 20)

Shiraz, Bannockburn (page 20)

Shiraz, Evans & Tate (page 71)

Shiraz, Peter Lehmann (page 68)

Shiraz, Palandri (page 74)

Shiraz, Tim Smith (page 14)

Shiraz Extra Special, Asda (page 71)

Shiraz, First Flight Reserve, Somerfield (page 76)

Shiraz, Heartland, Directors' Cut (page 12)

Shiraz Reserve, Belgravia (page 22)

Shiraz-Viognier, John Loxton/ Marks & Spencer (page 68)

Shiraz Wildcard, Peter Lehmann (page 44)

SPARKLING

Hardy's Crest (page 82)

❹ 2004 Tempranillo-Tannat, Bouza, Las Violetas, Canelones, Uruguay, £9.95, Great Western Wine

If this is the new face of Uruguay, hurrah! Uruguay has completely different growing conditions to the South American giants Chile and Argentina, and has struggled to find successful red wine styles that an export market might like. This splendid effort, from one of Uruguay's best independent producers, shows how to tame the fearsome Tannat grape yet not subdue its character excessively. The fruit is rich and round: half Tempranillo strawberry, half Tannat damson and plum. The perfume is half Tannat violet and half the toasted cashew of oak that Tempranillo sucks up so devotedly. And the tannin? Well, that's still mostly the rough kiss of Tannat, as raw and purple as any grape's tannin in the world. But it works.

❺ 2002 Cabernet Sauvignon, Kangarilla Road, McLaren Vale, South Australia, £9.99, Majestic Wine

Absolutely delightful Aussie Cabernet from slow-ripening, high-altitude vineyards on the edge of the fairly warm McLaren Vale, and this accentuates the perfume and juiciness of the wine. The fruit is wonderfully pure: ripe, sweet blackcurrant, as rich as you could want, scented with fresh mint and cocooned in cream.

❻ 2004 Sauvignon Blanc, Tamar Ridge, Tasmania, Australia, £9.99, Oz Wines

Sauvignon Blanc likes cool conditions, and Australia doesn't offer anywhere much cooler than Tasmania, the lovely island in the chilly waters south of the mainland. What's exciting here is that you get an aggressive style – rare enough for an Aussie Sauvignon – but you also get a full spectrum of green flavours, not just lean acidity. This has fistfuls of gooseberry and capsicum greenness, with a fair suggestion of green pea and asparagus – but rather more lime zest and lemon juice. And yet there's a reassuring ripeness to all this green flavour, like a stream of syrup softness flowing through the cool green jungle.

7 2003 Malbec, Ricardo
Santos, La Madras Vineyard,
Mendoza, Argentina, £7.99,
Majestic Wine

Argentina is good at fatness
in red wines; chubbiness,
squeezability. Some of the
supposedly fashionable red
wines are slathered with new
oak and have tannins that
make your gums cry 'ouch'.
But they go against what
Argentina does best: full, rich,
ripe, huggable reds. This has a
marvellous, deep, almost
syrupy quality that coats your
mouth with the sweetness of
cherry and plum and then
offers you just a suggestion
of scented mint and a lick of
brown sugar. Lush and lovely.

8 2004 Verdelho, Chapel
Hill, McLaren Vale, South
Australia, £7.99, Australian
Wine Club

Verdelho is a grape that Aussies often hold up as being a
natural successor to Chardonnay. It doesn't taste a bit like
Chardonnay. But its marked acidity allows the grape to thrive
in hot conditions like the McLaren Vale and still keep its
freshness. And Chapel Hill are the masters of Verdelho. This
has a lovely acidity that somehow seems gentle, just a nudge
in the ribs rather than a kick in the teeth – and it has a gentle
ripeness of honeysuckle, Bath buns, a touch of creamy yeast
and an aftertaste a bit like what you'd expect from the flower
of a pepper tree.

9 2003 Chardonnay, Chalker's Crossing, Tumbarumba,
New South Wales, Australia, £7.99, Anthony Byrne

Most of the currently fêted Aussie Chardonnays are coming
from the cooler corners of Australia, and this is no exception.
Tumbarumba is high in the Snowy Mountains down near the
Victoria border. It's pretty chilly down there, but the
Chardonnay grape loves it, and if you wanted an Aussie
Chardonnay that reminded you of white Burgundy, this might
be a good place to start, with its refreshing acidity, its
appetizing peach and oatmeal fruit, and toasty oak
savouriness of grilled cashew nuts.

Other Aussie reds

Badgers Creek, Aldi (page 80)
Cabernet Sauvignon, Chapel Hill (pages 61, 94)
Cabernet Sauvignon, Kangarilla Road (page 32)
Cabernet Sauvignon, Shady Grove (page 67)
Cabernet Sauvignon, First Flight, Somerfield (page 77)
Cabernet Sauvignon, Founder's Block, Katnook (page 36)
Cabernet Sauvignon, Wrattonbully Vineyard, Evans & Tate (page 64)
Cabernet Sauvignon-Merlot, Moda, Joseph (page 21)
Cabernet Sauvignon Reserve, Co-op/Katnook (page 70)
Cabernet Sauvignon-Shiraz, Lost Sheep, Evans & Tate (page 76)
The Fergus, Tim Adams (page 31)
Grenache, Thiele Road, Schwarz (page 22)
Grenache-Mataro-Shiraz, Tim Smith Wines (page 22)
Grenache-Shiraz, 'DNA', Tim Smith Wines (page 21)
Grenache, Peter Lehmann (page 92)
Malbec, Lizards of Oz (page 68)
Mighty Murray Red, Andrew Peace (page 50)
Ruby Cabernet-Shiraz, Sainsbury's (page 80)
Shiraz-Cabernet, Pondalowie (page 95)
Shiraz-Cabernet, First Flight, Somerfield (page 77)
Shiraz-Sangiovese, Il Briccone, Primo Estate (page 95)
Tryst, Nepenthe (page 64)
Zinfandel, Nepenthe (page 21)

SPARKLING
Rosé, Jacob's Creek (page 55)

⑩ 2001 Cabernet Sauvignon, Ruca Malen, Mendoza, Argentina, £8.75, Corney & Barrow
Fascinating big bruiser that manages to be assertive and brash as well as submissive and soft, all at the same time. The fruit is rich, sweet, verging on the overripe – but if you're in the right mood you'll say it's a hotchpotch of blackcurrant, black plum and mountain herbs ripened to perfection and coated in black chocolate. And then you notice a surprising, syrupy soft presence of ripe loganberry and raspberry.

⑪ 2004 Dolcetto d'Alba, Magna, Paolo Manzone, Piedmont, Italy, £7.50, Adnams
Dolcetto in Italian means 'little sweet one'. Don't you believe it. Most Dolcetto may flatter to deceive, with its come-hither, purple-pink hue and super-fresh smell, but it's generally pretty raw stuff. And this one's high acidity and turbid purple fruit shriek for food, but they shriek a lively tune – proud black fruit, raw-boned, like damson skins stripped of their flesh and flailed with slate, an earthiness of stark minerality. But with a plate of cured meats and sausages, it's wonderfully challenging and refreshing.

⑫ 2002 Old Vine Zinfandel, Bogle Vineyards, California, USA, £9.95, Great Western Wine
Clarksburg isn't a vineyard area of any great reputation; it's at the top end of California's white-hot Central Valley, where the Sacramento River snakes

towards San Francisco Bay. But being unheralded has meant no one bothered to rip up old Zinfandel vines in favour of Chardonnay or Merlot in pursuit of short-term profit. So when the world suddenly said, hey, we want something new and exciting, Bogle Vineyards were able to say, 'What about something old and exciting from our forgotten Zinfandel vines?' This is lovely, fat, red wine oozing with the good Zin flavours of dates and strawberries and raisins, and the masculine smell of polished leather riding boots.

⓭ 2001 Pinot d'Alsace, Beblenheim, Domaine Bott-Geyl, Alsace, France, £7.99, James Nicholson
When you see Pinot d'Alsace on the label – without the qualifying Blanc, Gris or Noir – it means you've got a mix of Pinot varieties, and this mix can be highly successful. Bott-Geyl is a serious producer, and this is lovely wine, quite unlike anything else from France, almost rich in its perfumed honeyed way, but refreshing fluffy apple flesh and a streak of mineral stoniness keep the balance perfectly.

⓮ 2003 Rioja Malvasia, Martin Cendoya, Heredad Ugarte, Spain, £7.99, Anthony Byrne
Malvasia is a smashing grape and used to play a major part in white Rioja. But nowadays the more adaptable, high-

Aussie whites

Chardonnay, Chalker's Crossing (page 33)
Chardonnay, Diamond Valley Vineyards (page 13)
Chardonnay, Wine Society/ Wirra Wirra (page 42)
Chardonnay, Moonambel, Dalwhinnie (page 25)
Chardonnay, The Olive Grove, D'Arenberg (page 98)
Chardonnay, Wayfarer, Hardys (page 79)
Chardonnay, Wildcard, Peter Lehmann (page 49)
Chenin Blanc, Peter Lehmann (pages 48, 96)
Riesling, Tim Adams (page 97)
Riesling, Sainsbury's/Geoff Hardy (page 75)
Riesling, Eaglehawk, Wolf Blass (page 77)
Riesling Limited Release, Brown Brothers (page 38)
Sauvignon Blanc, Adelaide Hills, Co-op (page 44)
Sauvignon Blanc, Ashbrook Estate (page 19)
Sauvignon Blanc, Tamar Ridge (page 32)
Sauvignon Blanc-Semillon, Cape Mentelle (page 97)
Sauvignon Blanc-Semillon, Sainsbury's/Capel Vale (page 71)
Sauvignon Blanc-Semillon, Suckfizzle (page 18)
Semillon, Tim Adams (page 12)
Semillon, Peter Lehmann (page 98)
Semillon, Estate Reserve, Denman Vineyards (page 70)
Semillon-Sauvignon Blanc, Pinnacle, Palandri (page 44)
Verdelho, Chapel Hill (page 33)

SPARKLING
Bird in Hand (page 53)
Jansz (page 100)

yielding Viura has largely taken its place. Thankfully there's still some left, because this is a remarkable lush white. You smell it and you think it's going to be too fat and woody to taste good, but these white Riojas have a magical way of marrying the most surprising flavours: here we've got custard tarts, strawberry, blood orange juice and the dust from under a carpenter's bench. Strange? Yes. Does it work? Yes. And will it age for another 5 years? Unbelievably, yes again.

---

⑮ 2004 Valdeorras Godello, Gaba do Xil, Telmo Rodríguez, Galicia, Spain, £6.99, Adnams

Godello is an excellent white grape from Spain's drizzly north-west. There's not a lot of it in Spain, but wine wizard Telmo Rodríguez has located a patch and made this delightful example, mellow and aromatic yet with an appetizing rasp that is part of the charm. You get a lovely flavour of apricots, but it's as though the skins have been rubbed with shiny grey stones. You get a delightful scent of lemon zest oil, but you also get the bitterness of the pith. Very interesting, very satisfying white.

---

⑯ 2002 Cabernet Sauvignon, Founder's Block, Katnook, Coonawarra, South Australia, £8.99, Bibendum

This is a strong, serious expression of Coonawarra Cabernet, itself probably Australia's most famous Cab. Many Coonawarra reds are immediately approachable, but this is a pretty massive wine for an area famed for so-called elegance. The fruit is dark and rich – loads of blackcurrant and black plum smeared with black treacle – but even this fruit-fest is almost hijacked by tannin and oak. Almost, but not quite.

---

⑰ 2003 Parcela #7 Reserva, Viña von Siebenthal, Panquehue, Aconcagua Valley, Chile, £7.95, Mayfair Cellars

North of Santiago, the Aconcagua Valley isn't particularly well-known as a wine region but the potential is clearly massive if this impressive red, from a mix of Bordeaux varieties (Cabernet Sauvignon, Merlot, Cabernet Franc), is anything to go by. This is powerful and serious but is still centred on beautiful blackcurrant fruit, eucalyptus scent and a creamy texture which gets the better of the tannins. Classic ripe, focused Chilean red.

---

⑱ 1999 Côtes du Rhône-Villages Sablet, Domaine le Souverain, Rhône Valley, France, £8.99, Maison du Vin

Sablet is a relatively unsung village in the southern part of the Côtes du Rhône. But over the past few years I've begun to rate it higher and higher, especially for the way it gives real character to the Grenache grape, which dominates the local

wines. 1999 was one of the years that first brought Sablet
recognition, and this excellent single-vineyard example shows
why: superripe red strawberry and cherry fruit now mellow
and mature, and a real sackful of maquis herbs, led by thyme
and rosemary, thrown into the vat. It's lovely now, but wines
like this can age for years yet.

**⑲ 2003 Syrah-Mourvèdre, Novas, Viñedos Orgánicos
Emiliana, Colchagua Valley, Chile, £7.95, Vintage Roots**
Powerful, serious wine from Alvaro Espinoza, one of Chile's
most exciting young winemakers and a great believer in
organic and biodynamic methods. The Syrah-Mourvèdre blend
is common in southern France but not in Chile, so get a
mouthful of this: dark, intense, tannic, but with tremendously
rich red plum fruit and loads of pepper and spice.

**⑳ 2004 Viognier Grande Réserve, Vin de Pays d'Oc,
Domaine Cazal Viel, Languedoc, France, £7.99, Thresher**
Viognier isn't supposed to be dainty and retiring. Its whole
raison d'être is that it can bring a lush, vivid apricot juicy fruit
to the party and, if you're lucky, heady floral scent and crème
fraîche fatness. Well, let's stick with the apricot here, because
we get it in spades – a lovely fat apricot jam texture, and a
dense flavour dominated by apricot, but backed up by peach
skin and pear. This is a powerful Viognier statement.

**㉑ 2003 Mâcon-La-Roche-Vineuse, Alain Normand,
Burgundy, France, £7.15, Christopher Piper Wines**
A delightful oddity from a village in the predominantly white
wine region of the Mâconnais. Most Mâconnais soil is
unsuitable for reds, but La Roche Vineuse soils are
predominantly limestone and granite, and Monsieur
Normand's 30-year-old Gamay vines produce a mild, mellow
red of ripe strawberry sweetness and leathery scent that
happily lies halfway between Beaujolais and Burgundy in style.

£5 to £7

We introduced an 'Under £7' section last year to try to remove the price point straitjacket, particularly from independent retailers who simply don't have the economies of scale which make it possible to massage and cajole – or bully – their prices into the £4.99 slot. In any case, £4.99 may be the battleground for supermarkets, but £5–7 is not so much the battleground as the playground for independents.

❶ 1999 Riesling, Brown Brothers Limited Release, Victoria, Australia, **£5.99**, Booths

What a delightful shock. I was knocked sideways by the intensity of lime zest and petrol aggression soothed into submission by cream and custard richness. Fantastic mature Riesling. Then I discovered the price: it's a steal. Try it if you can find a bottle.

❷ 2003 Côtes du Ventoux, Fayard, Domaine de Fondrèche, Rhône Valley, France, **£7.05**, Les Caves de Pyrene

Côtes du Ventoux is one of those slightly off-the-beaten-track areas of the southern Rhône – but it can be very good indeed. This is marvellous red: a dense superripe core of black plum and black cherry, with some baked dates from the 2003 heat, and an unusual scent of herbs: not just the usual bay and thyme, but creamy tarragon as well.

❸ 2004 Grenache-Viognier, La Croix Belle, Vin de Pays des Côtes de Thongue, Jacques & François Boyer, Languedoc, France, **£5.75**, Lea and Sandeman

Vin de pays is a designation often used for the less good patches of vineyard land in France's south, or as a label that allows growers to plant grapes not native to the area. Well, Côtes de Thongue really is good vineyard land. And Grenache and Viognier are really good southern grapes. This a smashing wine with a mellow autumnal quality, a waxy, sensuous texture from the Grenache and a superripe nectarine and pear flesh flavour, tickled with coriander spice and overlain with a hothouse floral scent.

❹ 2003 Mâcon-Chardonnay, White Burgundy, Cuvée Paul Talmard, Burgundy, France, **£6.99**, Adnams

If only all Mâcon-Villages were as good as this. It helps that it comes from a top producer, Talmard, who has vines in one of the Mâconnais' best villages, Uchizy. The result is a lovely, pure, ripe Burgundy, rich from the 2003 sun, with a full, fat apple weight, a dab of yeast and mouthwatering clean acidity. It finishes in true Burgundian style with creamy nut and honey washing over your tongue. Excellent.

---

❺ 2002 Cabernet Sauvignon, Peñalolén, Maipo Valley, Chile, £6.99, Oddbins

This is the younger brother of Domus Aurea (see page 11), and you can see the family resemblance, even in miniature. It's pretty deep red, and has a lovely lift of blackcurrant, chocolate, eucalyptus and mint. There's just a dash of coal smoke that smudges the effect, but it's a good, intense, blackcurranty Chilean Cabernet.

❻ 2001 Côtes du Roussillon-Villages Tautavel, Le Mascarou, Domaine des Chênes, Roussillon, France, £6.99, Lea and Sandeman

Only a few years ago, Côtes du Roussillon was usually dismissed as a place where the sun and wind baked all the life out of the grapes. But a new generation is showing that these wild areas have fantastic potential for wines that ooze with the fiery richness of the far south. This is surprisingly soft, with a rich blackberry fruit that becomes half-submerged in fudge – but it also has a pungent aroma of bay leaf and the acrid smoke of charcoal, and the whole thing throbs with raw energy.

Argentina

WHITE

Torrontes, Crios de Susana Balbo, Dominio del Plata (pages 40, 98)
Semillon-Chardonnay, Santa Lucia, Aldi (page 81)

ROSÉ

Syrah Rosé, Santa Julia, Familia Zuccardi (page 96)

RED

Bonarda, Catena Zapata (page 39)
Bonarda-Sangiovese, Santa Julia, Familia Zuccardi (page 92)
Cabernet Sauvignon, Ruca Malen (page 39)
Cabernet Sauvignon-Malbec, Catena Zapata (page 68)
Cheval des Andes (page 94)
Clos de los Siete, Michel Rolland (page 19)
Malbec, Ricardo Santos (page 33)
Merlot-Malbec-Cabernet Sauvignon, Dancing Monkey (page 48)
Sangiovese, La Agricola (page 78)
Shiraz, El Dueño, Bodegas Esmeralda (page 76)
Syrah, Trivento, Concha y Toro (page 73)
Tempranillo, Q Zuccardi (page 67)

---

❼ 2003 Bonarda, Alamos, Bodegas Catena Zapata, Mendoza, Argentina, £5.99, Booths

In its Italian homeland of Lombardy, Bonarda is virtually defunct. But in the sunsoaked plains of Argentina, it comes into its own. This wine has lashings of trademark wild strawberry sauce flavours, evident acidity and a tannic bite, but it comes together to make an unusual and delicious fruit-first red.

Spain

SPARKLING
Cava Brut Rosé, Codorníu (page 54)
Cava Brut Vintage, Roca i Amat (page 83)
Cava Brut Vintage (page 83)

WHITE
Almansa, Castillo de Almansa, Bodegas Piqueras (page 50)
Rioja Malvasia, Ugarte (page 35)
Rioja (barrel-fermented), Torresoto, CVNE (pages 66, 97)
Rioja (unwooded), Torresoto, CVNE (page 74)
Valdeorras Godello, Telmo Rodríguez (page 36)
Viña Sol, Torres (page 96)

ROSÉ
Valdepeñas Rosado, Viña Albali (page 96)

RED
Almansa, Marqués de Rojas, Bodegas Piqueras (page 42)
Garnacha, Vineyard X, Bodegas Borsao (pages 50, 92)
Garnacha-Tempranillo, La Riada, Bodegas Aragonesas (page 46)
Navarra, Santa Cruz de Artazu (page 25)
Rioja, Viña Caña (page 76)
Rioja, Bodegas Navajas (page 79)
Rioja Crianza, Conde de Valdemar (page 94)
Rioja, Cuvée Nathalie, Bodega Muriel (page 71)
Rioja Reserva, Viña Caña (page 72)
Rioja, Roda II, Bodegas Roda (page 18)
Rioja, Tomas Blanco Crespo, Telmo Rodríguez (page 64)
Tempranillo, Celtus, Viña Santa Marina (page 43)
Tempranillo, Dragon, Berberana (page 51)
Tempranillo-Merlot, Altozano, Somerfield (page 75)

8 2002 Cabernet Sauvignon, Winemaker's Selection, Veramonte, Maipo Valley, Chile, £6.99, Somerfield
Good, classic Chilean Cabernet. The Maipo Valley near Santiago is historically the best place to grow Cabernet, and this wine shows why: dense, serious texture and a fair thwack of tannin, but soaring above it all the sweet, sun-ripened rich blackcurrrant fruit of Chilean Cabernet on top form.

9 2004 Beaujolais, Jean-François Garlon, France, £7.05, Roger Harris
One of those delightful red wines that provides simple, predictable pleasure. Beaujolais should be about pleasure and nothing else. This has a heady scent of bananas and strawberries and a texture that teases your throat to open wide and down the wine in one go.

10 2004 Torrontes, Crios de Susana Balbo, Dominio del Plata, Cafayate, Argentina, £5.49, Anthony Byrne
Torrontes is one of those spicy, perfumy grapes that can be too much of a good thing if not carefully grown and handled. Cafayate, in the mountainous north of Argentina, is the perfect place to grow it. This wine is delicately sensuous, with peach blossom scent, pineapple chunk and honey richness and lime acidity, all in perfect balance, not at all overpowering, and deliciously easy to drink. *Also at Majestic Wine.*

Salud (*Sah-loo*)

'Fuego & Hielo'

ALTOS DE
TAMARON

RIBERA DEL DUERO

DENOMINACIÓN DE ORIGEN
PRODUCE OF SPAIN

'Fire & Ice'

ALTOS DE
TAMARON

Best buys

⑪ 2004 The Society's Australian Chardonnay, Wirra Wirra
♀ **Vineyards, McLaren Vale, South Australia, £5.75, The Wine Society**
It's interesting to see how this wine has changed over the years. As we have moved away from the original Aussie model of rich fruit and heavy oak to a fresher, less oaky style, so has The Society's Chardonnay. This is still full, with rather an attractive flavour of nectarine and pineapple and even a hint of Burgundian savouriness, but it is distinctly fresher and more acid-influenced than it used to be.

⑫ 2003 Cabernet Sauvignon, Errázuriz, Aconcagua Valley,
♦ **Chile, £5.99, Somerfield**
There aren't many wineries in the Aconcagua Valley, but Errázuriz has been there for donkey's years and established itself as one of Chile's leading wineries by making good, gutsy wines like this. It's packed with ripe blackcurrant fruit whose almost syrupy richness is balanced by tannin, eucalyptus scent and a lime zest acidity.

⑬ 2003 Almansa, Marqués de Rojas, Bodegas Piqueras,
♦ **Spain, £5.50, Averys**
Old vines are the key to red wine quality in this parched corner of Spain's high Castile plateau; the vineyards for this wine have been there since the Civil War in the 1930s. The grape, Garnacha Tintorera – which is not Garnacha at all, but another name for Alicante Bouschet – is unusual in that its juice is dark purple; it adds an intriguing medicinal depth to the rich, tasty blackberry and loganberry fruit which swamps your palate.

⑭ 2004 Sauvignon Blanc Reserve, Montes, Casablanca
♀ **Valley, Chile, £5.59, Majestic Wine**
Montes' reputation is as a producer of serious, powerful reds, but its whites seem to get better year by year, especially as they include more fruit from cool areas like Casablanca. This Sauvignon is nicely tangy, reasonably full in texture, but with all the desirable Sauvignon flavours – lime zest, nettles, kiwi fruit, coffee bean – there in force.

⑮ 2003 Pinot Noir, De Loach, California, USA, £6.95,
♦ **The Wine Society**
To get a Californian wine from a good winery like De Loach, using the trendy Pinot Noir grape, can't be easy. To get it at this price and of such good quality is a real achievement by The Wine Society's buyers. If you've seen the film *Sideways* but haven't yet sniffed and slurped your way through a Californian Pinot, this strawberry- and red cherry-flavoured example, soft but with a mineral streak, is a good place to start.

⑯ 2004 Unoaked Chardonnay, Errázuriz, Casablanca Valley, ♀ Chile, £6.99, Thresher

Errázuriz has been making really good, rather rich, oaked Chardonnay for some time, but this unoaked style is a new departure in response to our liking for less oak in our Chardonnay. It's a very modern, refreshing style, tasting of green melons and apple flesh, sharpened up by lemon acidity, but also with a nice plump feeling from being aged on its lees.

⑰ 2002 Blaufränkisch, Erwin Tinhof, Burgenland, Austria, ♟ £6.65, Savage Selection

Did you know Austria even *made* red wine? It does, and it's very tasty. This is a splendid stew of black cherries – and their skins and stones too – made thicker and richer with muscovado sugar, but tempered with freshly ground white pepper and the curious but refreshing green perfume of lily stems.

⑱ Plantation 1905, Marie-Claude & Jean-Louis Poudou, ♟ Languedoc, France, £6.25, Waterloo Wine Co

You'll notice on this wine's label that it's only a vin de table (France's lowest wine designation), so there's no vintage and it doesn't tell you where it comes from. It is vin de table because it is using grape varieties that are not allowed by the local authorities. It doesn't mean they're not *good*, they're simply forbidden. But one piece of information has sneaked on to the label – Plantation 1905. The vines are old. Seriously old, and it's age that can turn an ordinary vine variety, even a forbidden one, into something magic. And this wine is magic. It tastes like the skins rather than the flesh of really ripe fruits – and they're a wild bunch: rosehip and Scandinavian lingonberry mixing with black cherry and black plum, a little syrup and a smattering of herbs.

⑲ 2002 Tempranillo, Celtus, Viña Santa Marina, ♟ Estremadura, Spain, £5.75, Savage Selection

This comes from the far west of Spain, almost on the Portuguese border, and the wines are built in a hefty manner to match the local food. This is fairly tannic, but that wouldn't matter with food; it's got appetizing acidity, ripe strawberry and apple fruit and a creaminess that has the savoury edge of cream bought direct from the farm gate.

⑳ 2003 Merloblu, Castello di Luzzano, Lombardy, Italy, ♟ £6.49, Booths

Really good Merlots are hard to track down, since so many are made in a confected, over-commercial manner. But this one, from near Milan, is good, with rich plum and blackcurrant fruit, a nice nip of tannin and some tasty oak.

Under a fiver

£4.99 is the big battleground for the supermarkets and a lot of the big brands, who seem to think we all have a blind spot as soon as £5 flashes up in front of our eyes. This price point isn't so crucial for independent merchants, who can take the time to personally 'sell' wines to their customers. I've found lots of good stuff at around a fiver, though most of it comes from the high street.

❶ 2004 Viognier, Cono Sur, Colchagua Valley, Chile, **£4.99, Waitrose**
Cono Sur is a Chilean winery on a roll at the moment, and a lot of its wines sell for less than a fiver. This is delightful stuff: full, apricoty, with a touch of marmalade bittersweetness and refreshing lemon sherbet acidity.

❷ 2004 Carmenère, Los Robles, Fairtrade, Curicó Valley, Chile, **£4.99, Co-op**
In January I went to the Los Robles co-operative where this wine is made, and was moved by how much good Fairtrade prices can do in a deprived community. So, if you buy this wine I can assure you your money is helping wipe out poverty in this part of Chile. And it tastes good – rich, soft black fruit, scoured by freshly ground black peppercorns and scented with lilies. *Also at Sainsbury's, Somerfield, Waitrose.*

❸ 2004 Semillon-Sauvignon Blanc, Pinnacle, Palandri, Western Australia, **£4.99, Waitrose**
Western Australia has made the Semillon-Sauvignon blend a speciality, and this example does it beautifully. It's ripe and relatively soft, but packed with green apple flesh and lime and kiwi greenness to make a very refreshing mouthful with just a hint of mellow autumn ripeness.

❹ 2002 Shiraz, Wildcard, Peter Lehmann, South Australia, **£5.03, Budgens**
You can always trust Peter Lehmann to come up with ace value for money wines. This is like a top Shiraz in miniature – good full blackcurrant fruit, plum syrup and chocolate richness, scented with leather and a little eucalyptus. *Also at Co-op, Oddbins.*

❺ 2003 Cabernet Franc, Touraine, Atlantique, Donatien Bahaud, Loire Valley, France, **£4.99, Co-op**
Everyone tells me it's difficult to sell Loire reds – yet it shouldn't be: they are some of France's breeziest, most

LOS ROBLES

'MUCH MORE THAN A GREAT GLASS OF WINE.'

Says Oz Clarke
of the Los Robles Carmenère

Guarantees
a **better deal**
for Third World
Producers

FAIRTRADE

Los Robles wines are available from Sainsbury's,
Somerfield, Waitrose and leading independents.

refreshing styles. So if you've not tried one yet, dive in with this bright raspberry flavoured yet stony, dry, herb-scented perfect picnic red from the broiling 2003 vintage.

❻ 2004 Colombar-Chardonnay, Firefinch, Springfield Estate, ♀ Robertson, South Africa, £4.99, Booths

This comes from the top-quality Springfield Estate, and sneaks under the £5 barrier because it uses the unsexy Colombard grape. But Colombard performs really well in the heat of South Africa. Very fresh, slightly yeasty dry white with mild but refreshing lemon acidity and a hint of lemon blossom scent.

❼ 2004 Garnacha-Tempranillo, La Riada, Campo de Borja ♥ Bodegas Aragonesas, Aragón, Spain, £4.99, Thresher

These juicy, peppery reds from Spain are becoming a bit of a Thresher speciality. Great! Because they're just the kind of fruit-packed wines you can drink anytime, anywhere. This is piled high with syrupy strawberry fruit and strewn with pepper and herbs.

❽ 2003 Primitivo-Merlot, Da Luca, IGT Tarantino, Puglia, ♥ Italy, £5.03, Budgens

Pretty powerful stuff, this, dark and bitter-edged. But that's how wines should be from Italy's far south: laden with chocolate and plum ripeness, restrained by a snap of tannic toughness yet finishing up gentle and rich.

❾ 2004 Viognier, Vin de Pays d'Hauterive, Domaine de la ♀ Bastide, Languedoc, France, £4.99, Booths

This wine actually comes from the Corbières region of France's far south, better known for brawny, herb-strewn reds. Well, they can clearly make Viognier too, because this has a floral scent, lovely soft apricot fruit, and a lot more freshness than many Viogniers achieve.

❿ 2004 Pinot Noir, Cono Sur, Rapel Valley, Chile, £5.03, ♥ Budgens

Cono Sur Pinot Noir has been the best-value Pinot Noir in our market for years: soft, rather glyceriny, mellow and easy to glug. There seem to be different cuvées of 2004 around – some of the others are good, yet surprisingly peppery – but this is soft, gently smoky and full of strawberry fruit, just the same as usual.

⓫ 2004 Fiano, Inycon, Sicily, Italy, £4.99, Booths

♀ Italy is full of unusual and tasty red grape varieties, but we're now seeing some really interesting ancient white varieties making a belated appearance. Fiano is one of these,

VIÑA ALBALI

A lovely drop of wine.

*"Gran Reserva 1997.
Arguably the best value-for-money Spanish wine
for the past 20 years"*

John Radford, Wine International

*"Reserva 1999.
Lovely soft, oak-scented wine with
a splash of blackcurrant juice"*

Oz Clarke's Best Buy Under £5

For more information contact Free Run Wines. Tel: 01672 540990
or email: info@freerunwines.com

and the wine is fresh, gentle, with a mild apple and pear fruit
– mainstream flavours, yet this wine's personality has an
indefinable 'something else' that makes it special.

12 2003 Merlot-Malbec-Cabernet Sauvignon, Dancing
Monkey, Mendoza, Argentina, £4.99, Oddbins
Dancing Monkey is a new brand Oddbins has brought over to
the UK; it shows Argentina could do really well at £4.99 – if
the wineries thought hard enough about what we wine
consumers really like. Well, I like this – lots of plummy fruit, a
refreshing stony dryness and even a whiff of perfume.

13 2003 Viognier, The Boulders Limited Release, California,
USA, £4.99, Co-op
Viognier seems to be popping up all over the place. This one's
from California and, as you'd expect from the sunny Golden
State, the wine is fat and rich with gooey apricot and peach
fruit and an attractively syrupy texture.

14 2004 Chenin Blanc, Peter Lehmann, Barossa Valley, South
Australia, £5.03, Budgens
You don't see much Australian Chenin, but it's a grape that's
ideally suited to the warm Aussie conditions, because it keeps
good acidity even when the sun shines relentlessly. This is a
good, full mix of fresh apple and honey and a touch of Danish
pastry softness. There's lemon, too – lemon juice and a lemon
zest scent. Nice now, it'll age for years. *Also at Co-op, Waitrose.*

> *'...fresh apple and honey and a touch of
> Danish pastry softness...lemon, too'*

15 2003 Douro, Valtorto, Portugal, £5 on special offer, Averys
Strong, direct, uncompromising stuff, not for faint-hearts. Big,
fat, black plum fruit mixes with a dose of black pepper and
some apple peel acidity to create a good, tub-thumping red.

16 2002 Syrah, Vin de Pays d'Oc, Herrick, Languedoc, France,
£4.99, Budgens
This started out years ago as a lovely scented Syrah, then lost its
way. Now it's back, without the scent, but with lots of juicy,
squashy dark fruit and a wraith of smoke hovering over the glass.

17 2003 Nero d'Avola, Inycon, Sicily, Italy, £4.99, Booths
Nero d'Avola is a smashing Sicilian grape variety – it's been
there hundreds of years, but we are only just now seeing

For more wine recommendations see Oz Clarke's Wine Style Guide, pages 92–101

wineries work out how to make the best of it. This is full and rich and just a tiny bit rough – nicely rough, though, with great wodges of plum, black cherry and sultana fruit and herb scent to brush aside the appetizing bitter edge.

'...nicely rough, with great wodges of plum, black cherry and sultana...and herb scent'

---

18 **2004 Mâcon-Villages, Chardonnay, Cave de Prissé, Burgundy, France, £4.99, Waitrose**
Mâcon-Villages is often too expensive for what it is – a nice, simple, refreshing unoaked Chardonnay. But this one hits the spot at the right price, with good apple fruit, peach-skin and tobacco perfume and a soft, creamy aftertaste.

---

19 **2004 Sauvignon Blanc, Oracle, Western Cape, South Africa, £4.99, Oddbins**
Very fresh, yeasty young Sauvignon with apple fruit, and lemon peel and green leaf acidity. There's just a hint of sweetness, but this is a nice drink. The Oracle Chardonnay is good too.

---

20 **2003 Chardonnay, Wildcard, Peter Lehmann, South Australia, £5.03, Budgens**
Peter Lehmann is probably Australia's most trustworthy and consistent value-for-money expert. This is a full, tropical, rather figgy and pineappley Chardonnay, but it's done in a restrained manner, so it works. *Also at Co-op, Oddbins.*

Under £4

This is really the supermarkets' area of strength, but we found some very pleasant stuff at under £4 – so here it is.

1 **2004 Minervois, Château Villerambert-Moreau, Languedoc, France, £3.99, Booths**
They don't come better than this at £3.99. It's one of those wines you can serve at a smart dinner party – hey, it's got a Château name on the label for goodness' sake – and imply it cost twice as much. But why would you? Brag about what a fantastic bargain it is – and let its outstanding juicy flavours of plum and damson, lit up by lily scent and roughened a fraction by pepper, speak for themselves.

Best buys

❷ 2003 Garnacha, Vineyard X, Bodegas Borsao, Campo de Borja, Aragón, Spain, £3.99, Thresher

Nowhere in Europe does juicy, crunchy, bargain reds better than Spain, and Thresher has been enthusiastically promoting these wines for several years. This is a challenging, satisfying mouthful of squashy strawberry syrup fruit and pepper bite with a hint of a rasp from some herbs as well. If you buy three, you only pay for two, which takes the price down to £2.66.

❸ 2004 Domaine de Pellehaut, Vin de Pays des Côtes de Gascogne, South-West France, £3.99, Booths

This won one of the top prizes in the 2005 Vins de Pays competition – and I can see why. It's wonderfully fresh, yet reassuringly soft: green apples, blackcurrant leaves and lemon zest, wrapped in cotton wool. Lovely.

> '...top Vin de Pays...wonderfully fresh, yet reassuringly soft'

❹ 2004 Mighty Murray Red, Andrew Peace, South Eastern Australia, £3.98, ASDA

Call a wine 'Mighty Murray' – I can see him now, a burly, muscular jackaroo but with a feminine side – and I want a big wodge of flavour, too. I certainly get all of this here. Dark red, loaded with plum and strawberry and a splash of blackcurrant, and churned up with mint and herbs and some good masculine earth. And it's *not* sweet. We want more basic Aussie reds like this.

❺ 2004 Cape White, Obikwa, Adam Tas Cellars, Western Cape, South Africa, £3.99, Oddbins

South Africa does this style very well – apple and green melon fruit, sprinkled with summer dust and stones, and sharpened up with lemon juice. Very nice Sauvignon-like style, for not much money.

❻ 2004 Almansa, Castillo de Almansa Colección Blanco, Bodegas Piqueras, Spain, £3.99, Booths

Almansa is a hot, high, arid region just to the east of the vast La Mancha plateau in central Spain. Its chief role historically has been making powerful, tongue-numbing reds to beef up feebler brews from elsewhere. But the Piqueras winery is an ambitious, skilful operation that is revolutionizing both whites and reds. This is a lovely modern white: full, dry, soft, not fruity, but with an appetizing undertow of bark and stones that is very refreshing.

❼ 2003 Tempranillo, Dragon, Berberana, Viño de la Tierra de Castilla, Castilla-La Mancha, Spain, £3.99, Budgens

Back to what Spain does increasingly well – a rich, chunky red full of ripe plum fruit with just a nip of tannin to keep your palate alert and a touch of creamy oak to round out the flavour.

❽ 2003 Shiraz, Crow's Landing, California, USA, £3.99, Co-op

With the dollar as weak as it is, we really should be seeing more decent cheap Californian wines over here. Well, the Co-op has been the most successful high street operation at sourcing wine from the Golden State for years. This is a good, full, stewy, jammy red – plums with a hint of prune and a dollop of soothing toffee cream to round it off. Not classic Shiraz, but they're learning.

❾ 2004 Pinot Grigio, Nagyrede, Hungary, £3.79, Booths

Hungary has so much to offer in the white wine world, but we still seem unwilling to take her seriously. Well, if you're a Hungary virgin, there's no better place to fling off your inhibitions than here, and down a glass of this gentle, mellow, apple- and toffee-scented, almost dry delight.

❿ 2004 Sauvignon Blanc, Riverview, Hungary, £3.99, Waitrose

This is a real star turn from Hungary. They've been making top Sauvignon Blanc for at least 10 years, but the price stays relentlessly low. Frankly, they'd like to push the price up, but we won't pay. OK then, let's buy more of what they've got at this price – and for really good, snappy, gooseberry and blackcurrant leaf and green apple Sauvignon with a real tang to it, this can't be beaten.

> *'...good, snappy Sauvignon with a real tang to it'*

⓫ nv Chilean Red, Santa Clara, Viña Requingua, Curicó Valley, Chile, £2.99, Booths

Very attractive basic red: simple, juicy, red plum fruit and a spoonful of soy sauce savouriness and floral scent from the inclusion of some Carmenère grapes in the blend.

⓬ 2004 Cuvée Fleur, Vin de Pays de l'Hérault, Languedoc, France, £3.55, Waitrose

Pink wine sales are way up this year and there's a fair amount of good stuff around. This lively, quite full, almost fat wine mixes strawberry fruit with melon, apple and pear freshness.

Fizz

The quality of many Champagnes seems to be on the up this year: the last two or three years have offered better blending quality than the pretty dire 2001, which formed the basis of a lot of non-vintage blends last year. But when it comes to classic flavours, well, clearly Sussex is the place to look, because for sheer class and pleasure, nothing could knock Ridgeview off the perch it proudly occupied last year.

❶ 2000 Cavendish Brut, Ridgeview, West Sussex, England, £19.60, Jeroboams

I bang the drum for English fizz at every possible opportunity: I use it in wine tastings and on broadcasts, I take it abroad – and the thrilling thing is, people *always* love it. The less thrilling thing is, a large number of them give it the Victor Meldrew 'I don't *believe* it' treatment. So the battle isn't yet won, but with the consistent brilliance of producers like Ridgeview and Nyetimber (see page 81), it can't be long before we put aside our frankly absurd belittling of things vinous and English and acclaim our top producers for what they are – producers of some of the best sparkling wines in the world. So *do* drink English! And start here – with the gorgeous yet restrained flavours of hazelnuts and brioche, the fruit of a big juicy baked apple and a soaring acidity that carries the tiny bubbles to every corner of your mouth.

❷ nv Champagne Brut Blanc de Blancs, Grand Cru, Cuvée Pierre Moncuit-Delos, France, £17.25, H & H Bancroft

If I had to choose one village in Champagne that consistently produces the most delicious grapes, I think it would be Le Mesnil, tucked into the slopes of Champagne's main Chardonnay area, the Côte des Blancs. The Chardonnay from Le Mesnil always seems to have a special purity about its flavour – and it's Le Mesnil Chardonnay that made this wine. It's positively lush in style for Champagne, but it cries out with

typical Champagne acidity before a variety of soft flavours
spread across your palate – syrupy yeast, sponge cake and
brioche, ripe apple flesh and just a hint of Horlicks malted milk.

❸ **nv Champagne Brut Numéro 2, Philizot & Fils, France,
£15.99, Irma Fingal-Rock**
Good characterful Champagne, made from the black grapes
Pinot Noir and Pinot Meunier grown at the family vineyards in
the Marne Valley. It has a full, nutty, yeasty character, and fruit
like a rustic apple crumble – and it's pretty full-bodied too.

❹ **nv Champagne Brut, Premier Cru, Pierre Vaudon,
Union Champagne, France, £17.45, Haynes Hanson & Clarke**
Year in year out, one of the most predictably enjoyable
Champagnes on the market. This wine, from Avize at the
southern end of the Côte des Blancs, is full and gentle, with a
welcoming aroma of crème fraîche and breakfast brioche,
clean apple fruit and the promise of nutty depth if you leave
the bottle under the stairs for a year.

❺ **nv Champagne, The Wine Society's Private Cuvée,
Alfred Gratien, France, £17.50, The Wine Society**
This is made for The Wine Society by the small, quality-
conscious Alfred Gratien company, who make some of the
best Champagnes I've tasted over the years. This is a little
young (Gratien, even non-vintage, can benefit from 5–10 extra
years in bottle), but the quality is there, with a bright acidity
that reminded me very slightly of lime and ginger, very
attractive apple fruit and a nutty yeast finish.

❻ **2001 Bloomsbury, Ridgeview, West Sussex, England,
£14.99, Waitrose**
Here's another star from Ridgeview, one of England's world-
class fizz producers. It's a few quid cheaper than the
Cavendish (left) and is more widely available, but it's still
outstanding wine, with an exquisite balance between
foaming youth and discreet maturity, soft apple flesh streaked
with lemon acidity, soothed and stroked by a delightful
blossomy oatmeal and honey yeast. *Also widely available.*

❼ **2004 Sparkling Pinot Noir, Bird in Hand, Adelaide Hills,
South Australia, £12.80, Tanners**
This is white wine made entirely from black Pinot Noir grapes,
which gives a fuller texture than if a white grape like
Chardonnay had been included in the blend. It's full of bouncy
fresh banana and pear fruit that could almost be too much if
it weren't for the invigorating foamy cascade of bubbles that
accompanies it.

❽ 2001 Montlouis Brut, Cray, Loire Valley, France, £7.99, Flagship Wines

Montlouis is next door to Vouvray in the Loire Valley, but the vineyards are cooler. Which in some years in the Loire can mean very cool indeed. But that's no great problem for fizz, because the best sparkling wine is made from grapes that are barely ripe. This one has loads of strong appley fruit, good yeast richness and an attractively assertive acidity.

❾ nv Champagne Brut Rosé, Fleury Pére et Fils, France, £21.75, Vintage Roots

Organic fizz. Since it rains half the time in Champagne I don't know how they manage to do without anti-rot sprays, but evidently they do, and the result is this fairly high-toned and acidic wine with a good splash of apple, pear and strawberry fruit. It's still a bit young, but the fruit is attractively ripe.

❿ nv Cava Brut Rosé, Pinot Noir, Codorníu, Spain, £7.99, Majestic Wine

Attractively mature – most pink fizz is released too young – with a good rich sense of strawberry fruit and apple mellowness and an appetizing, rather stony, dry streak.

⓫ nv Prosecco, La Marca, Cantine Sociali della Marca Travigiana, Veneto, Italy, £5.99, Waitrose

Prosecco is a supremely undemanding wine style. Prosecco's bubbles should flare briefly in the glass then fade – but by then you'll have gulped it down and be ready for a refill. And you'll find this pretty easy to gulp, with its bright, soft apple

> **2003 Lambrusco Rosso Secco, Concerto Reggiano, Medici Ermete, Emilia-Romagna, Italy, £6.49 Booths, £7.38 Les Caves de Pyrene**
>
> I just couldn't resist including this, but it's such a whacky wine I thought we'd better put it in a box of its own. If you've always thought Lambrusco was an excuse to hit the auto-eject button – sweet and limp and almost devoid of alcohol – that's not the real thing. *This* is the real thing, drunk in vast quantities by Italy's most serious eaters, the good burghers of Emilia-Romagna. They love it – and so do I – because it cuts brilliantly through the rich Bolognese cuisine. This is purple, dark, dry – yes, dry – but not raw or rasping. It has the mouthwatering acidity of a damson, or a sweet-sour cherry, and it's got the half-wine, half-fruit flavour of bruised apples, pears and plums. Add just a hint of tannin, and I can imagine the Parma hams of the region leaping from their perches and begging to be sliced and eaten alongside it.

and pear fruit, a slight orange perfume and a mild earthy undertow coated in cream.

⑫ nv Sparkling Rosé, Jacob's Creek, Australia, £7.84, ASDA
What a nice surprise! Really good, yeasty, strawberry-fruited, foaming pink of true quality from one of Australia's commercial giants. *Also at Waitrose.*

Fortified & sweet wines

I couldn't exactly say that the fortified wine market in the UK is buzzing, and nor is the market for dessert wines. But there are a lot of fascinating flavours about if we are prepared to take time out from a diet of Sauvignon and Shiraz and delve into a calmer, more ancient wine world where the flavours demand contemplation and reflection.

❶ Oloroso Solera 1842, Valdespino, Spain, £11.99/half bottle, Waitrose [DRY]
This wonderful wine describes itself on the label as 'rich sweet oloroso'. That's like calling the Houses of Parliament a Parish Hall. In fact I'm not sure there's anything sweet at all about this tantalizing nectar. Rich, yes, but a richness tempered by sourness and bitterness that comes from laying down a selection of barrels in 1842 and then letting the elements of earth and wind, heat and cold and the passing of time push the liquid further and further from what might well once have been merely rich and sweet. When I first tasted it I wrote 'it's like being clubbed on the head as I gaze out to sea.' What did I mean? I still don't know. 'It's so good I can't write a decent tasting note' was my conclusion. What I can tell you that it's as deep and intense as anything you'll ever place in your mouth, and the flavours that attack you begin with the bitter blackness of French chocolate, of espresso coffee beans, of Guinness, of blackened toast; then brown takes over from black – burnt muscovado sugar, brown leather sofas, chestnut brown, dates and treacle brown, balsamic vinegar brown, sour and rich and distantly smelling of smoke from a fire of kindling cut from a scented forest.

❷ Manzanilla Mariscal, Dolores Bustillo Delgado, Spain, £6.70, Tanners [DRY]
Dry sherries are some of the greatest bargains to be had in the world of wine – all that craftsmanship, the delicacy and skill required to bring one of the most fragile of wines to

maturity, the years of careful watching and waiting and blending as the wine matures in its barrels from being a young, bland, ditchwater-dull table wine to to this unique drink. The fruit – if I can call it that – is ice cold, as though all the flesh and the sugar has been sucked out and just a shivering memory remains. And in place of fruit we have a gaunt cadaver of acidity that pads itself out with a fleeting richness of bread yeast, slightly sour crème fraîche, brioche mixed with fragments of brazil nut and salt. If you've never tasted great dry sherry, be prepared for a flavour like no other.

---

❸ 2002 Maury, Domaine des Schistes, Roussillon, France, £14.25, Berry Bros & Rudd [SWEET]

Maury, down near the Pyrenees, used to be a backwater of tired old sweetish brown wines. There was nothing wrong with the grapes – from 80-year-old Carignan vines and Grenache vines over 50 years old – but the winemaking was in a time warp until a new generation took over the estates in these windswept hills and hauled the wine styles into the 21st century. This is brash but beautiful, heady at 16% – but not at all spirity – and wonderfully easy to drink too much of, packed as it is with strawberry and cherry and raspberry sauce sweetness, cut through with a glistening shaft of mineral, stony dryness and a swirl of black pepper scent. If you've ever wondered what to drink with chocolate ... here's the answer.

> *'...if you've ever wondered what to drink with chocolate'*

---

❹ 1997 Scheurebe Eiswein, Darting Estate, Ungsteiner Hönigsäckel, Pfalz, Germany, £12/half bottle, Marks & Spencer [SWEET]

Eiswein is a very rare wine style. It is a risky wine to make: you may well lose your whole crop, because you have to wait way into winter for a really serious frost to freeze the grapes solid on the vine, massively concentrating the sugar and acidity. If the frost doesn't come – and many years it doesn't – your grapes simply rot into an unusable slime. But clearly the frost did come in 1997. This is a beautiful pure essence of the Scheurebe grape with just a suggestion of maturity. There's an unctuous rich pink grapefruit syrup sweetness, abetted by a lanolin waxiness and restrained by the high acidity typical of Eiswein.

For more wine recommendations see Oz Clarke's Wine Style Guide, pages 92–101

❺ Viejo Oloroso, The Society's Exhibition, Sanchez Romate, Spain, £9.95, The Wine Society [DRY]

You look at the dark chestnut brown just fringed with green, you smell the black treacly pungency, and you think this must be sweet. But it's not. It's intensely, searingly, penetratingly dry. The flavours do appear rich and brown – hazelnut syrup, black treacle, essence of black chocolate and ripe figs and raisins – but with all the sugar surgically removed. Instead you get an incredibly powerful assault on your taste buds, the raw essentials of flavours, unadorned with sweetness, though seasoned with balsamic vinegar and the meatiness of a fresh-crumbled Oxo cube. I'm not sure when you drink it – sitting down is the very least I can recommend – but drink it you must for a unique experience.

> '...hazelnut syrup, black treacle, chocolate... but with all the sugar surgically removed'

❻ 2002 Saussignac, Cuvée Flavie, Château des Eyssards, South-West France, £11.73/50 cl, Flagship Wines [SWEET]

Saussignac is near Bergerac, up the Dordogne Valley, and the grapes are 80% Semillon (the same as Sauternes) and 20% Chenin Blanc (that's a Loire Valley grape). Whatever, this is a classic sweet wine of France's South-West, rich with the sweetness of cling peaches and pineapple chunks in syrup, perfumed with ginger and apricot blossom, and as fat and satisfying as waxy lanolin coated with crème fraîche.

❼ Manzanilla La Gitana, Bodegas Hidalgo, Spain, £5.99, Majestic Wine [DRY]

Probably the best of the widely available dry sherries. Bone dry, perhaps a little softer than the Mariscal (see page 55) but with the same seaside savouriness that all manzanilla should have, the same disturbingly appetizing scent of white bread yeast and hazelnut and savoury cream and the same veiled threat of a gaunt acidity hovering at the back of your palate.

❽ 1999 Tokaji Aszú 5 Puttonyos, Oremus, Hungary, £24/50 cl, The Wine Society [SWEET]

Don't expect an easy ride with this. Tokaji is barely a tamed animal at the best of times, and this wine has something of the Magyar bear straining to be unleashed. But it doesn't quite slip its lead. Even so, there is a strange 'oldness' about the wine – as though all the autumn fruits have been left a little too long on the bough and the sweetness ends up as a syrup of bletted medlars, bruised apples and windfall goldengages. There is a kind of pastry softness, but it's like an apricot Danish made out of sourdough, topped with crystallized pineapple and burnt caramel and briefly splashed with tomato-skin acidity. Do I like it? By itself, not awfully, but with strong cheese or foie gras, probably very much.

❾ 1999 Dow's Crusting Port, Portugal, £13.99, Oddbins [SWEET]

Crusting Port is an excellent halfway house between a mellow though tasty Late Bottled Vintage and the full-on power of a Vintage Port. Lighter batches of wine from two or more vintages are blended together, then bottled early so that they mature in bottle. This means the wine develops good dark blackberry and black cherry fruit and a silky texture as well as a little peppery reminder that this is strong stuff. It reaches maturity twice as fast as Vintage Port, and costs half as much. *Also from ASDA, Tesco, Waitrose.*

> *'...halfway between a mellow LBV and the full-on power of a Vintage Port'*

❿ 2003 Coteaux du Layon, Clos de Sainte Catherine, Domaine des Baumard, Loire Valley, France, £21.25, Jeroboams [SWEET]

Classy sweet Loire wine, very attractive now, but it will be far deeper and richer and more exciting if you leave it for 10 years. Yes, 10 years: that's really the minimum these Loire classics need to show their spurs. So, wait if you can, but if you can't, this is already a lovely wine, scented with honeydew melon and peach blossom, streaked with refreshing acidity and tasting of pears and peaches – with the promise of quince jelly and honey in years to come.

⓫ Dry Oloroso, Solera Jerezana, Diego Romero, Spain, £6.55, Waitrose [DRY]

This was a star wine a few years ago. Then it got sweetened up and lost its star quality. Now it's fairly dry again, and it's got its bite back, its sense of burnt nuts and singed caramel and a dry syrup of figs and buttered brazils. It hasn't yet quite recovered its former brilliance, but it's on the way.

⓬ Moscatel Superior, Emilín, Lustau, Spain, £7.95/half bottle, Berry Bros & Rudd [SWEET]

They grow a little Moscatel (the Spanish name for Muscat) in the sherry region and this is a good example: fat, sweet, tasting of dates and sultanas and crumbled crystallized brown sugar. But there's also a streak of mineral stoniness that keeps it from cloying. *Also at Averys.*

CARMEN

You can´t talk about passion.
　　　　You have to taste it.

Pinot Grigio 75cl
Only **£3.79**
£3.79 per 75cl

Ile La Forge Merlot 75cl
Only **£4.99**
£4.99 per 75cl

Chianti 75cl
Only **£3.49**
£3.49 per 75cl

Don't pay through the nose for good quality wines

Crianza 75cl
Only **£3.29**
£3.29 per 75cl

Cremant Du Jura 75cl
Only **£5.49**
£5.49 per 75cl

Claret 75cl
Only **£3.29**
£3.29 per 75cl

Spend a little Live a lot

Supermarket superstars

As news of mergers, takeovers and shutdowns of supermarkets continues to swirl around the business pages, it would be easy to look on the black side and gloomily predict that we shall soon be seeing less and less choice of wines from fewer and fewer companies. Yet when the giant Tesco can stock supreme wines like Tim Adams Semillon (page 13) and Chapel Hill Cabernet (below) and have them available in over 500 stores, things don't seem so bad. And when Safeway disappears into Morrisons' hands, but one side effect is that Waitrose buys some of the 'redundant' Safeways and you can now get Waitrose products as far north as Lancashire and Yorkshire, you might even raise a cautious cheer. So we've looked on the bright side and found some fantastic wines – genuine supermarket superstars – only 5 of our top 20 are over £10. That's not exactly a scenario of doom.

Please bear in mind that wine is not made in infinite quantities – some of these may well sell out, but the following year's vintage should then become available.

❶ 2000 Cabernet Sauvignon, Nativa, Carmen,
Maipo Valley, Chile, £7.99, Waitrose
Every time I taste this gorgeous wine I find it difficult to believe there is a more beautiful Cabernet anywhere in Chile. No. Anywhere in the world. And it's doubly exciting because of its price: £7.99. For the essence of Cabernet, where beauty gets the better of power, where sheer enjoyment gets the better of intellectual appraisal. Cabernet isn't often like that. But this is pure blackcurrant, distilled into a syrup of sweetness and balance, with a couple of mint leaves crunched into the liquid and the wine stopped from cloying by a distant dryness – as though it had been filtered through summer-warmed stones.

❷ 2001 Cabernet Sauvignon, Chapel Hill, McLaren Vale/
Coonawarra, South Australia, £9.99, Tesco
Although Cabernet is the grape, it comes from two areas of South Australia a couple of hundred kilometres apart and with completely different personalities. The Cabernet shines through beautifully, but an extra thrill comes from seeing how the power of the warm-climate McLaren Vale fruit deals with the fragrant, more delicate cool-climate fruit of Coonawarra. Brilliantly is the answer. The wine is seriously dry and dense, with a dark, brooding, licorice heart balanced by a heavenly scent of blackcurrant and blueberries and a soothing toffee softness.

Supermarket selection

❸ 2003 Pinot Noir, Lone Range, Craggy Range, Martinborough, New Zealand, £13.99, Marks & Spencer

Wow! They say New Zealand is the next best place for Pinot Noir after Burgundy. Well, including Burgundy, if they go on making stuff like this. It comes from a single vineyard in Martinborough, at the very bottom end of the North Island, which some experts reckon is New Zealand's best patch of dirt for Pinot. This is marvellously self-indulgent, with a rich viscous texture and strawberry fruit so ripe it's dropping from the bush. There's just a brush of herbs to stop you completely losing your self-control. But why hold back?

❹ 2003 Touriga Nacional, Quinta da Fonte Bela, Estremadura, Portugal, £5.99, Tesco Finest

Fantastic value for money. It's made by Jose Neiva, one of Portugal's top winemakers, and uses what people call Portugal's top red grape, Touriga Nacional. This is smashing stuff: unusual, very Portuguese in its richness and individuality, with a lovely perfume of spiced buns and eucalyptus and a riproaring flavour of chocolate and sweet yet sharp blackcurrants. You won't get that for £5.99 from anywhere but Portugal.

❺ 2003 Sauvignon Blanc, Floresta, Santa Rita, Leyda Valley, Chile, £9.99, Waitrose

The only thing wrong with this wine is a rather silly heavy bottle. Why? The last thing that Sauvignon should be doing is weighing us down. Sauvignon's job is to snap our brains and our palates wide awake, to slake our thirsts and set our taste buds drooling for more. And the wine *inside* the silly bottle does just that. The grapes were grown in Leyda, a cool new region out on the coast that is rapidly establishing itself as Chile's best Sauvignon site, and this has all the thrilling ice-cold grapefruit acidity, nettle and blackcurrant leaf scent and gooseberry and green pepper crunchy flavour that you could wish for.

❻ 2004 Pinot Noir, Secano Estate, Viña Leyda, Leyda Valley, Chile, £6.99, Marks & Spencer

If Leyda is making waves for Sauvignon, it's cranking up the volume for Pinot Noir as well. This is a single estate wine with a superb, lush texture from what can only be a young vineyard – there were no vines at all in the Leyda Valley a few years ago. It has a fabulous winsome balance of fruit and acidity and a delicious cream and strawberry flavour that reminds me of strawberry blancmange.

For more wine recommendations see Oz Clarke's Wine Style Guide, pages 92–101

Another corking year.

Waitrose has won many more of the major wine awards than
any other supermarket. The reason isn't hard to find. We have
more Masters of Wine than any other supermarket. We have a
range of no less than 650 wines. And we have wine specialists
on hand in branches to guide our customers. The fact is, at
Waitrose we take our wine very seriously. And you can enjoy
the fruits of our labour by visiting any branch or
waitrose.com/wines.

Supermarket selection

❼ 2002 Zind, Zind-Humbrecht, Alsace, France,
♀ £13.99, Waitrose

This is vin de table, the lowest designation of any French
wine. Well, that's because Olivier Zind-Humbrecht thinks that
the wine laws that control Alsace are asinine, so he said, I'll
make whatever wine I want and label it as a basic plonk. But
that £13.99 price tag tells you this is superior kit – a
challenging and super-appetizing wine, strongly mineral in
style, the stones mingling with a slightly smoky sweat and
luscious honey to make a dense, almost opaque white.

---

❽ 2003 Cabernet Sauvignon, Wrattonbully Vineyard,
♀ Evans & Tate, South Eastern Australia, £6.99, Marks & Spencer

Here's a deep, powerful Cabernet from Wrattonbully; not a
very appetizing name, but these limestone areas north of
Coonawarra could become some of South Australia's best. The
flavours they produce are concentrated and serious, packed
with redcurrant acidity and blackcurrant depth and an almost
Italian black chocolate bitterness.

---

❾ 2004 Tryst, Nepenthe, Adelaide Hills, South Australia,
♀ £7.29, Waitrose

A tryst is a meeting between lovers. Well this is a probably
undreamt-of relationship between French Cabernet, Spanish
Tempranillo and Californian Zinfandel. The Cabernet gives
eucalyptus scent and ripe Rosa plum fruit, with the plum
skins adding an acidity that Tempranillo's strawberry fruit and
Zinfandel's fudge date richness cope with effortlessly. But it's
a threesome. Now, that *is* illicit. Even in Australia.

---

❿ 2002 Rioja, Tomas Blanco Crespo, Telmo Rodríguez, Spain,
♀ £7.99, Marks & Spencer

M & S liaise with Telmo Rodríguez, one of Spain's best young
winemakers, for this Rioja, and he's made an excellent job of it
in the difficult year of 2002. You can sense the grapes were
less than perfectly ripe from their peppery texture, but hold
the wine in your mouth a moment, and it slowly evolves to a
lovely glycerine richness of loganberry and strawberry sauce.

⓫ 2001 Amarone della Valpolicella Classico, Vignale,
♀ Veneto, Italy, £13.99, Waitrose

Amarone is one of those wines it's difficult to taste blind,
because the whole point of the wine is its brooding depth, its
wild flights of sour acidity and unexpected scents – and its
bitterness. Bitterness is why it's called Amarone. This is a good
example. It has a great slab of black chocolate at its heart, but
that's swimming in a cauldron of beef stew with a good splash
of balsamic vinegar and sloe wine. Strange, but excellent.

Please
Do
Not
Disturb

WHAT
IS A
TRYST

?

NEPENTHE

TRYST
CABERNET·TEMPRANILLO·
ZINFANDEL
2004
ADELAIDE HILLS, AUSTRALIA

⑫ 2002 Riesling Spätlese, von Hövel, Scharzhofberg,
Mosel-Saar-Ruwer, Germany, £9.99, Waitrose

Don't give up on German wine! I beg you! I know the
Germans made a frightful mess of their reputation by
swamping our wine stores with dire Liebfraumilch and
Piesporter, but the thing to remember is that Germany
doesn't do cheap wines very well – it's too cold and wet. But
there are special sites all over Germany, protected from the
elements, exposed to the midday sun, where unique wines
are produced. Scharzhofberg is one of these, a steep, slithery
slope of decomposed slate that you can actually taste in the
wine itself, which is very low in alcohol – 7.5% – and slightly
spritzy, and the slate chill cuts through the confectioner's
cream and honeyed apple crumble fruit with a vibrant acidity
like Bramley apple skins.

⑬ 2003 Côtes de Castillon, Seigneurs d'Aiguilhe,
Château d'Aiguilhe, Bordeaux, France, £7.99, Waitrose

Every vintage this wine is an absolute beauty. 2003 was
extremely hot and many wines taste overtannic and baked,
but despite not having quite the 'classic' Bordeaux character
it possesses in cooler years, this is still an impressive
mouthful of superripe damsons, plums and blackberry fruit
marginally touched by overripeness.

> *'every vintage this wine is*
> *an absolute beauty'*

⑭ 2004 Sauvignon Blanc, Clocktower, Wither Hills,
Marlborough, New Zealand, £9.99, Marks & Spencer

Marks & Spencer has cleverly persuaded Brent Marris, one of
New Zealand's trendiest Sauvignon producers, to create this
snappy white for them. He lives up to his reputation with a
wine that's like a compendium of green flavours – capsicum
and asparagus, gooseberries and lime zest – all bathed in a
syrupy ripeness and dotted with coffee beans.

⑮ 2003 Rioja (barrel fermented), Torresoto, CVNE, Spain,
£6.99, Marks & Spencer

If you want rich flavours in your dry white wines, but don't
like Chardonnay any more, then barrel-fermented white Rioja
presents you with a fascinating alternative, with its almost
overpowering mix of custard apple and sharp lime fruit, its
nutty depth and its coating of slightly burnt Bird's custard.
The back label says consume within 1 year. Sure you can. But
this wine will go on getting deeper, wilder and more
wonderful for a good 10 years.

⑯ 2001 Meursault, Burgundy, France, £18.99, Tesco Finest

♀ Meursault is such a popular wine that it's not easy to obtain a decent quality for an own label, but Tesco has managed it. From a cool and not very popular vintage (2001) they've found this full, gentle, oatmealy, nutty white of lovely viscosity and appealing youth. I'd give it another couple of years of aging.

⑰ 2000 Cabernet Sauvignon, Shady Grove,

♥ Clare Valley, South Australia, £13.99, Marks & Spencer

M&S is not exactly giving this away, but it's a top drop of Aussie Cabernet and beautifully mature at over 5 years old. That explains the rich, mellow texture and it also explains how the blackcurrant fruit is understated yet rich and persistent, and the eucalyptus and mint scent is intertwined yet never dominates.

⑱ 2002 Tempranillo, Q Zuccardi, Mendoza, Argentina,

♥ £9.99, Tesco

'Q' is the top label produced by the charming José Zuccardi and 2002 is his best vintage yet. Tempranillo is the Rioja grape from Spain, but it takes on muscles when it gets to Argentina. This dark beast has tannin to spare, but richness that measures up to the challenge, a richness of licorice and prunes and plum that's tempered by herbs and an acidity of stewed cranberries, then boosted by an oakiness that mixes savoury butter with coconut.

⑲ 2003 Chardonnay, Rustenberg, Stellenbosch, South

♀ Africa, £9.99, Waitrose

The fruit for this wine is fantastic, although there's also a funky note to it that might not be to everyone's liking. But if you get past that, you'll find exceptionally full, ripe peach, apple and pineapple fruit, an irresistible Sunday morning toast and butter fragrance and a viscosity that somehow stays refreshing through all the complexity of flavour.

⑳ 2004 Merlot-Carmenère-Cabernet Sauvignon, Trio,

♥ Concha y Toro, Rapel Valley, Chile, £5.99, Co-op

The winemaker's objective here is to create the best texture he can. Blending three grapes on purpose rather than by historical accident is still a new concept in Chile, but it really works, with each grape adding a little milk chocolate here, some soy sauce savouriness there, good dry blackcurrant and black plum fruit, even a sprinkling of herbs – but the lingering flavour is of all of them mingling together rather than one being dominant. Serious, classy red for only £5.99.

High street heroes

There's a fantastic choice of wines here, with countries like Austria and Canada joining the usual New and Old World suspects. And along with memorable flavours, there's really good value for money to be had – not one of these wines is over £10.

❶ 2004 Grüner Veltliner, Moosburgerin,
♀ **Weingut Felsner, Kremstal, Austria, £7.99, Waitrose**
Austria produces some of Europe's most delightful wines and the Grüner Veltliner grape in particular is wonderfully refreshing. Some grapes, like Sauvignon Blanc, have 'green' flavours. Grüner Veltliner has 'white' flavours: white apple flesh – including the core and the pips, but not the skin – white peppercorn, white radish. Add good acidity, a soft texture and a sensible alcohol level of 12.5% and you've got an undiscovered jewel.

❷ 2002 Malbec Reserve, Lizards of Oz, Kirrihill, Clare Valley,
♀ **South Australia, £6.99, ASDA**
Malbec is becoming quite well known in Argentina, but here's an example from Australia. It has a core of black cherry fruit, even a little blackcurrant, but to find it you'll have to fight your way through a bizarre and challenging hotchpotch of tobacco and plum skins, linseed oil, pepper, ginger and mint.

❸ 2002 Shiraz, Peter Lehmann, Barossa Valley, South
♀ **Australia, £7.99, Waitrose**
Peter Lehmann always gives you quality. He never overcharges. Overdeliver? He invented the phrase. He simply couldn't conceive of giving you at least a little bit more than you'd paid for. Well, here's his Shiraz. It's packed with chocolate, vanilla, black plum and raspberry with a whiff of herbs. It's serious hedonistic stuff. *Also at ASDA.*

❹ 2003 Cabernet Sauvignon-Malbec, Catena Zapata,
♀ **Tupungato, Mendoza, Argentina, £5.99, Marks & Spencer**
Excellent, dense, powerful wine, showing the serious, quality of Mendoza's best and coolest vineyards. The texture is pretty burly, but the wine is bulging with concentrated viscous damson and black plum fruit rich enough to cope.

❺ 2003 Shiraz-Viognier, John Loxton Regional Selection
♀ **Currency Creek, South Australia, £7.99, Marks & Spencer**
The supremely trendy mix of red Shiraz and white Viognier (everybody's doing it, but not always well). Currency Creek is

Best wine under the sun.

HARDYS

The best of Australia since 1853

In 1853, Thomas Hardy started crafting wines that would soon be prized in markets all around the world. Five generations later, the Hardys winemakers are still making the best of the rich soil and abundant sunshine of Australia's best regions to produce the current family of wines. A range that, without a shadow of a doubt, best expresses our founder's principles of quality, flavour and consistency.

www.hardys.com.au

quietly famous for subtle but confident flavours – nothing flashy, nothing brutal. Here, you've got it. Ripe blackberry fruit, but not intense, almost harking back to red loganberry, but the syrupy softness and the mix of toasty oak and honeyed, peachy Viognier makes you pretty happy with the fruit, red or black.

---

❻ 2004 Semillon, Estate Reserve, Denman Vineyards, ♀ Hunter Valley, NSW, Australia, £7.99, Tesco Finest

'Gosh. Tastes of leather and fish oil' isn't a cry that will impel many wine drinkers towards the glass – but those are the kinds of flavours you get in Hunter Semillon. In fact this one's got custard too – and a distinct whiff of farmyard to trade cudgels with a bright lemon acidity. That's Hunter Semillon. No one said you had to like it.

> *'...Hunter Semillon.*
> *No one said you had to like it'*

---

❼ 2003 Pinot Noir, Highfield Estate, Marlborough, New ♥ Zealand, £9.99, Tesco Finest

A vast improvement on the 2002 vintage. Dry, and just on the underripe side, but with very attractive gentle strawberry fruit, a nip of tannin and a pleasant lick of oak.

---

❽ 2003 Cabernet Sauvignon Reserve, Coonawarra, South ♥ Australia, £5.99, Co-op

This is made at the Katnook winery in Coonawarra, an area famous for producing some of Australia's leafiest, most blackcurranty reds. This won't disappoint – it's got a luscious blackcurrant jam fruit richness with just enough leafy green acidity and an ankle-bite of tannin.

---

❾ 2002 Pinot Noir, Five Vineyards, Mission Hill, Okanagan ♥ Valley, British Colombia, Canada, £7.99, Sainsbury's

An adventurous buy for Sainsbury's – a Pinot Noir from the mountain eyries of British Columbia in Canada. Well, they say Pinot likes cool conditions, so why not? And this has a positively viscous ripe texture to coat your palate, although the flavour of toast and strawberry and a little cream is altogether more wispy and mountain mild.

---

❿ 2003 Chablis, Cave des Vignerons de Chablis, Burgundy, ♀ France, £6.99, Somerfield

It's funny, but despite Chablis being a cool northern outpost

For more wine recommendations see Oz Clarke's Wine Style Guide, pages 92–101

of Burgundy, you don't want too good a ripening season, because the chilly, reserved style of the wine can only be achieved when the grapes really struggle to ripen. They raced to ripeness in 2003, but this wine has held on to its reserve, its earth and herb and lemon juice dryness.

---

⑪ 2004 Sauvignon Blanc-Semillon, Classic Selection, Capel Vale, Pemberton, Western Australia, £6.99, Sainsbury's

Pemberton is a cool-climate region in the south of Western Australia, and it shows in the wine, with good green capsicum, nettle and blackcurrant leaf sharpness yet a surprisingly tender texture that makes for very easy drinking.

---

⑫ 2002 Rioja, Cuvée Nathalie, Bodega Muriel, Spain, £5.99, Co-op

You don't normally look to Rioja for power, but this is seriously powerful red, with a rich, fat, dark fruit flavour of plums stewed in their skins, cinnamon spice, and a swirl of leather and refreshing acidity to round things off. This really needs 2–3 years, but it's good now.

---

⑬ 2002 Shiraz, Extra Special, Barossa Valley, South Australia, £6.98, ASDA

This is relatively restrained for a Barossa Shiraz: quite a few of these have taken the 'big is beautiful' mantra to a rather obscene, overblown conclusion that makes them just about OK to taste but too much of a behemoth to swallow. This has good blackberry fruit, syrup softness and an attractive black chocolate bitter bite, all in just about the right proportions.

---

⑭ 2003 Shiraz, Langhorne Creek, Evans & Tate, South Australia, £5.99, ASDA

Evans & Tate is a fairly big company and here it is doing a commendable job using its considerable fruit resources to offer us good flavour at a good price. This isn't massively rich, in fact it's quite lean in texture, certainly not superripe, but the scent of lilac stems and the mix of black plum, peppercorn, spice and a soft centre make it a charming drink.

---

⑮ 2002 Cabernet Sauvignon Reservado, Anakena, Alto Rapel, Requinoa, Chile, £5.99, ASDA

Anakena is one of Chile's go-ahead wineries, so well done ASDA in picking up this wine. Despite having strong blackcurrant fruit – really juicy and rich – this isn't a typical mainstream Cabernet, because it also has an intriguing scent of mint and sage and an aftertaste that mixes perfume and bitterness like when you chew on a sprig of fresh rosemary.

Chilean reds

Cabernet Sauvignon, Anakena (page 71)

Cabernet Sauvignon, Domus Aurea (page 11)

Cabernet Sauvignon, Errázuriz (page 42)

Cabernet Sauvignon, Peñalolén (page 39)

Cabernet Sauvignon, Nativa, Carmen (pages 61, 94)

Cabernet Sauvignon Reserve, Haras de Pirque (page 22)

Cabernet Sauvignon, Winemaker's Selection, Veramonte (page 40)

Cabernet Sauvignon-Carmenère, Doña Dominga, Casa Silva (page 74)

Carmenère, Cielo de Luz (page 79)

Carmenère, Gracia de Chile (page 72)

Carmenère, Los Robles (page 44)

Chilean Red, Santa Clara, Viña Requingua (page 51)

Merlot, Sainsbury's (page 79)

Merlot, Tesco (page 74)

Merlot-Carmenère-Cabernet Sauvignon, Trio, Concha y Toro (page 67)

Merlot, Cuvée Alexandre, Casa Lapostolle (page 16)

Merlot, Santa Lucia, Aldi (page 80)

Parcela #7 Reserva, Viña von Siebenthal (page 36)

Pinot Noir, Cono Sur (page 46)

Pinot Noir, Morandé (page 76)

Pinot Noir, Las Brisas Vineyard, Viña Leyda (page 94)

Pinot Noir, Secano Estate, Viña Leyda (page 62)

Shiraz, Sainsbury's (page 77)

Syrah-Mourvèdre, Novas, Viñedos Orgánicos Emiliana (page 37)

⑯ 2004 Carmenère, Gracia de Chile Reserva, San Alfonso Estate, Maipo Valley, Chile, £5.99, Co-op
This wine doesn't really do Carmenère's typically savoury side, but it does have rich black fruit oozing with damson syrup, and the texture is sweet and soft to match attractive toasty oak.

⑰ 1999 Rioja Reserva, Viña Caña, Spain, £7.99, Somerfield
This Rioja keeps getting better. It has lots of vanilla scent along with a cedarwood austerity; the flavour of red plums and strawberries mixed with savoury cream and cedar is serious, but highly desirable. You could age it a few years if you wanted to.

⑱ 2003 Gewurztraminer, Francis Klee, Alsace, France, £6.99, Tesco Finest
What a delight to find an unashamed, voluptuous, scented Gewurztraminer under a supermarket own-label. This wine is overflowing with the heady midsummer scent of tea rose and violets and its texture is as rich as Nivea Creme and as lush as lychees.

⑲ 2001 Châteauneuf-du-Pape, Les Vignerons des Dentelles Vaucluse, Rhône Valley, France, £9.99, Somerfield
Châteauneuf-du-Pape hardly ever appears for under a tenner nowadays, so this is a pleasant surprise. It's not a typically broad and weighty example – in fact it's a bit nonconformist, with warm strawberry and slightly overripe

cherry fruit and a strong resinous herb flavour of pine needles and thyme plucked from the garrigue. And I like it.

⑳ 2001 Valpolicella Classico, Vigneti di Montegradella,
Veneto, Italy, £5.99, Tesco
Fascinating red made by a method called 'ripasso', where the new wine is passed over the partially dried skins of overripe grapes: this causes a slight refermentation. The result is a rich, deep red, glyceriny wine with sweet cherry ripeness and an appetizing balsamic vinegar streak of sourness.

Chilean whites
Chardonnay, Asda/Viña San Pedro (page 80)
Chardonnay (unoaked), Errázuriz (page 43)
Chardonnay-Viognier-Marsanne, Novas (page 98)
Chardonnay, Winemaker's Lot, Concha y Toro (page 97)
Gewurztraminer, Winemaker's Lot, Concha y Toro (page 99)
Sauvignon Blanc, Viño Ulmo, (page 78)
Sauvignon Blanc, Floresta, Santa Rita (page 62)
Sauvignon Blanc, Garuma Vineyard, Viña Leyda (page 16)
Sauvignon Blanc Reserve, Montes (page 42)
Viognier, Cono Sur (page 44)

Economy class

Five quid – or £4.99 – is a massive battleground for wine. We don't buy kippers or butter or coffee solely on price point – but a lot of people *do* seem to buy wine that way. Consequently there's a lot of pressure on quality here. Many of the better-known brands that sell for £4.99 really don't stack up on flavour and value for money. But there is good stuff out there – and you won't go wrong with any of the wines I've listed below.

❶ 2003 Syrah, Oak-aged, Trivento Reserve,
Concha y Toro, Mendoza, Argentina, £4.99, Somerfield
This is the business. A lot of Argentinian wine at around this price lacks focus and personality, and a lot of Argentinian Syrah – or Shiraz – lacks excitement whatever the price level. Chile's biggest winery, Concha y Toro, clearly looked over the Andes and thought they could do better. Too right. This is deep, rich Syrah, serious, powerful, but never losing sight of its dark sweet heart of ripe plum and blackberry fruit, wrapped in cream toffee and chocolate and lightly rubbed with leather.

Supermarket selection

2 **2002 Shiraz, Palandri, Margaret River, Western Australia,**
£4.99, Waitrose
This is Palandri's basic Shiraz – they do more expensive ones
that I look forward to trying, but I hardly need to, this is so
tasty. Excellent blackberry and blackcurrant fruit laced with
licorice and spice and smoky melted chocolate.

3 **2003 Cabernet Sauvignon-Carmenère, Old Vines,**
Doña Dominga, Casa Silva, Colchagua Valley, Chile, £4.99,
Sainsbury's
Carmenère really does add an extra dimension when you
blend it with Cabernet or Merlot. This wine has a lovely fat
texture it couldn't have achieved by using Cabernet on its
own, and it certainly couldn't have achieved the magnificent
juicy mishmash of blackcurrants and black chocolate, mint
and pepper that the two grapes together achieve.

4 **2003 Rioja, Torresoto, CVNE, Spain, £4.99, Marks & Spencer**
The label says this wine is unwooded – well it doesn't taste
unwooded: there seems to me to be a subtle but successful
addition of oak influence, which has created the classic white
Rioja flavours of custard and pastry softness scythed through
by green apple acidity and the eye-popping scent of lime zest.

5 **2004 Chilean Merlot Reserve, Central Valley, Chile**
£4.99, Tesco
Delicious, ripe, rich red wine. Chile does this style so well and
for £4.99 there's some really top fruit being piled into the vat.
And they've sneaked in some Carmenère – you can taste it –
that irresistible jumble of black plum and blackcurrant fruit,
that savoury depth as though someone's splashed in some
soy sauce, and the lily and pepper tree perfume.

> *'Chile does this style so well...*
> *irresistible blackcurrant fruit'*

6 **2004 Sauvignon Blanc, Adelaide Hills, South Australia,**
£4.99, Co-op
Adelaide Hills is an expensive place to grow grapes, so the
Co-op has done really well in seeking out this mouthwatering
but gentle Sauvignon, with its bright melon, apple flesh and
pear fruit and mild lemon acidity and mineral rasp.

7 **2004 Soave Classico, Zenato, Veneto, Italy, £4.99, Waitrose**
Because of the flood of rubbish Soave that used to threaten to
drown us, we forget that Soave *Classico* – that Classico is
important – comes from lovely high-quality vineyards which

just need a bit of TLC. This isn't bursting with flavour like a Sauvignon Blanc – that's not what Soave does. But it *has* got a gentle waxy texture, soft apple and dusty peach-skin fruit and a minerally, zesty aftertaste that's pretty satisfying.

❽ 2003 Petite Sirah, The Boulders, California, USA, £4.99, Co-op

This seems to get better every time I taste it. There's been a dire shortage of any decent grog from California at £4.99 – most of the big brands are feeble beyond belief – so this is doubly welcome. Big, powerful, tannic – it really is crying out for a decent juicy T-bone steak – but with lots of blackberry sweetness mixed with custard softness and the scent of tobacco and honey.

❾ 2003 Tempranillo-Merlot, Altozano, Castilla y Léon, Spain, £4.99, Somerfield

This tastes like a milder version of Ribera del Duero – and that's one of Spain's priciest and most serious reds. This is still pretty serious, it's even a bit tannic, but the tannin gets washed away by a tide of blackcurrant and black plum syrup, and creamy, almost buttery oak barrel richness.

❿ 2003 Zinfandel, Californian Reserve, Jeff Runquist, USA, £4.99, Tesco Finest

Zinfandel grows all over the place in California – particularly in the boiling hot Central Valley. Well, these Zin grapes are from the Central Valley, but at the north end, where conditions are cooler, and the result is better wine – gentle in texture, with loads of slightly baked date and raisin and blackberry fruit and a touch of tobacco scent.

⓫ 2001 Brindisi Rosso, Cellino San Marco, Puglia, Italy, £4.99, Morrisons

You can taste the heat in this wine, but that's OK – it comes from way down in the south of Italy. You'd be a bit worried if you couldn't taste the heat. And the wine has managed to keep a surprising amount of perfume, so you get a slightly sun-baked damson and plum core of flavour, lifted and brightened by floral scent.

⓬ 2003 Australian Riesling, Geoff Hardy, South Australia, £4.99, Sainsbury's

Australian Rieslings are usually significantly more expensive than this – especially when they are top examples by respected producers. Which is exactly what this is. It's tangy

For more wine recommendations see Oz Clarke's Wine Style Guide, pages 92–101

in a citrus, lime zest way, with just a whiff of petrol about it – and that can be a surprisingly attractive extra element in a wine – and gentle, slightly peachy richness. If you've never tried Aussie Riesling, start right here.

'tangy, citrus, lime zest...with an attractive whiff of petrol'

⑬ 2004 Pinot Noir, Morandé, Casablanca Valley, Chile, £4.99, Marks & Spencer
Casablanca Valley is a popular and expensive place to grow grapes, so well done Marks & Spencer for getting hold of a class act like this for only £4.99. It's very pleasant Pinot – easygoing, mellow, with gentle strawberry and cream fruit to soothe any tannin-battered palate.

⑭ 2003 Shiraz, First Flight Reserve, South Eastern Australia £4.99, Somerfield
Everything you could want a £4.99 Aussie Shiraz to be: rich, chocolaty, pruny, with a sort of jam stew weight and a blackberry aftertaste. Good stuff.

⑮ 2003 Rioja, Viña Caña, Spain, £4.49, Somerfield
You won't find much Rioja at £4.99, so this is a welcome stalwart. it's quite gutsy for a Rioja, and not particularly soft and creamy, as many Riojas are, but it has an attractive black peppercorn and lily scent, strawberry fruit and a tasty mineral dryness a bit like graphite.

⑯ 2004 Shiraz, El Dueño, Bodegas Esmeralda, Mendoza, Argentina, £4.99, Marks & Spencer
Lots of rich, ripe Shiraz fruit – something you don't always get with Argentinian Shiraz – a decent slap of tannin, and some rather pleasant black plum and damson scent – something you quite often *do* get in Argentine reds, but they're usually made from Malbec.

⑰ 2004 Cabernet Sauvignon Rosé, Misiones de Rengo, Rapel Valley, Chile, £4.99, Somerfield
Pink wine! But you can really taste the Cabernet – blackcurrant leaf and blackcurrant fruit – and with a zippy acidity and a slight prickle on the tongue, it makes for a smashing glugger.

⑱ 2003 Cabernet Sauvignon-Shiraz, Lost Sheep, Evans & Tate, South Eastern Australia, £4.99, Marks & Spencer
Evans & Tate is a medium-sized operation with feet in both Western and South Eastern Australia, and this Cabernet-Shiraz

combines some of the herb dryness of Western Australia with the ripe black plum and blackcurrant of the states further east. It's the kind of satisfyingly tasty drink that the bigger Aussie brands should be producing for £4.99 – but they're not.

⑲ 2004 Vin de Pays du Gard, Saint Roche, Domaine de Tavernel, Languedoc, France, £4.99, Waitrose
Big, powerful, burly but balanced dark fruit stew, probably owing its pepper and hillside herb rasp to the Carignan grape and its thick wodge of black plum and blackcurrant fruit to the Merlot and Cabernet parts of the blend.

⑳ 2004 Riesling, Eaglehawk, Wolf Blass, South Eastern Australia, £4.99, Sainsbury's
Good, soft, slightly chubby Riesling with attractive lemony perfume just delicately splashed with petrol.

Everyday drinking

It was the wide spread of countries that pleased me most about these wines. It's that global wine glut being intelligently hoovered up by our high street wine buyers, with Somerfield and ASDA doing the hardest work and achieving the best results.

❶ 2003 Shiraz-Cabernet Sauvignon, First Flight, South Eastern Australia, £3.99, Somerfield
An excellent example of what own label should be all about. Loads of blackberry and black plum fruit, a spicy toastiness too, some attractive earthy roughness and appetizing tannin with a sweet, ripe black fruit finish. Well done Somerfield.

❷ nv Chilean Shiraz, Central Valley, Chile, £3.49, Sainsbury's
Seriously good Shiraz that could easily command a higher price. It manages to be powerful yet mellow at the same time – there's definitely a scratch of tannin there, but you need it when you have a wine as rich and ripe as this, overflowing with blackberry and black plum fruit, toffee richness, and the barbecue scent of grilling meat.

❸ 2002 Cabernet Sauvignon, First Flight, Murray Darling, South Eastern Australia, £3.99, Somerfield
More from Somerfield's excellent First Flight label. This time it's a straight Cabernet, and once again, it's showing loads of personality for £3.99. It's even got some maturity: it's 3½ years old. The flavour is powerfully blackcurranty and the fruit

really pings at you and is made even more focused by quite a high acidity. Put a scratch of herbs and a lick of tannin with that and you've got a seriously tasty glass of red.

---

❹ 2004 Sauvignon Blanc, Viño Ulmo, Lourdes,
♀ **Central Valley, Chile, £3.49, Marks & Spencer**
A bit gentle for Sauvignon Blanc, but Chilean versions usually are at the softer, riper end of the Sauvignon spectrum. It works because the flavour is all Sauvignon – coffee beans, green apple peel and a hint of lime zest.

---

❺ nv Hearty Red, Portugal, £3.99, ASDA
Bags of personality for less than £4. Portuguese reds have got so much personality we should all be drinking them more often. It's quite tannic, it's even a bit rustic – but it has a great wodge of licorice and syrupy boiled sweets and mint toffee, so I reckon a touch of the rustics doesn't do much harm.

---

❻ 2004 Chenin Blanc, Oak Aged, Western Cape, South
♀ **Africa, £3.99, Co-op**
Very attractive style of Chenin that South Africa can do so well. Gentle flavour of nuts and honey, even a little oatmeal, and a full spicy texture.

---

❼ nv Sauvignon Blanc, Vin de Pays du Jardin de la France,
♀ **Vinival, Loire Valley, France, £3.62, ASDA**
I like the lowish alcohol in this (11.5%). It probably means some of the crop was picked unripe, but that's exactly what you want if you're after a snappy, crisp Sauvignon Blanc. This has a good, assertive taste of green apple flesh and blackcurrant leaves, yet the texture is far from harsh.

---

❽ 2003 Chianti, Casa Laora, Tuscany, Italy, £3.49, Aldi
You don't expect Chianti to be a gentle, juicy Lucy kind of wine – and this one isn't. But it *isn't* the kind of iron filings battery acid that cheap Chianti can be. In fact, it's almost soft for a Chianti, but you'll have to gird yourself up for a mouthful of stewed strawberry and tomato mixed with a splash of balsamic vinegar soothed by cream toffee and a handful of herbs. Mmmm. That sounds like Chianti!

---

❾ 2003 Argentine Sangiovese, La Agricola, Mendoza,
Argentina, £3.99, Somerfield
Sangiovese is the Chianti grape, but it tastes different in the land of the giant sirloin. You still get the strawberry sauce and the balsamic vinegar, but with them you get banana freshness, some savoury cream and a blast of tannin that definitely shouts out for a slab of red-blooded steak

⑩ nv Rioja, Bodegas Navajas, Spain, £3.99, Morrisons,
🍷 This isn't top Rioja, but then £3.99 isn't a top Rioja price. What you get is pretty decent stuff – a suggestion of strawberry, a splash of creamy oak and a fleeting whiff of pepper.

---

⑪ 2004 Pinot Grigio, Western Cape, South Africa, £4.49,
🍷 **Co-op**
Pinot Grigio in Italy usually means almost no flavour and rather more money than you really want to pay. But Pinot Grigio is a smashing grape if you allow it to perform. This isn't ambitious, but it does have a mild but appealing flavour of apple flesh and lemon zest and just a touch of beeswax to fatten it up.

---

⑫ 2004 Chardonnay, Wayfarer, Hardys, South Eastern
🍷 **Australia, £3.98, ASDA**
There's a lot of tripe on the back label about wayfarers and voyagers and the original Mr Hardy's noble ambitions in life, but this is quite good commercial Aussie Chardonnay – slightly sweet but with decent pear and banana fruit and a fleck of spice flavour.

Bargain basement

There's still lots of good glugging grog to be had at around £2.99. So there should be – there's a massive global glut of wine and quite a bit of it's half-decent stuff. Chile and Australia offer the best buys at the moment, but there's some OK stuff from Europe too. As for suppliers – well you expect Aldi to do the bargain basement reasonably well – and they do. Morrisons and Sainsbury's are the best of the rest.

❶ 2004 Carmenère, Cielo de Luz, Central Valley, Chile,
🍷 **£2.99, Morrisons**
Welcome back, bargain basement superstar. A Morrisons Carmenère won this section last year, too. Cheap blends often change – and usually for the worse – but this is still a superb mouthful of deep, scented blueberry and blackberry fruit with the teasing perfume of a pepper tree in bloom. It shows you *can* do quality at this price if you want to.

---

❷ nv Chilean Merlot, £3.29, Sainsbury's
🍷 This wine was scrabbling for first place in this section last year – and it's still delivering the same powerful blast of rich red plum and strawberry fruit, scented with clove and cinnamon. Another triumph for quality and consistency.

❸ 2004 Australian Ruby Cabernet-Shiraz, South Eastern Australia, £3.19, Sainsbury's

Ruby Cabernet is a rough old grape, but when you sweeten it up with juicy Shiraz – then only charge just over £3 for it – you create another star bargain. This is chunky, stubborn, assertive stuff, with a growling undertow of beef tea, tea leaves and grape skins to rouse and rile the dark fruit. Glugger with grunt.

❹ 2004 Chilean Chardonnay, Viña San Pedro, Central Valley, Chile, £2.97, ASDA

Reliably enjoyable cheap Chardonnay: not sweetened up, not dumbed down, just good refreshing melon and apple fruit, lemon acidity, and a perky hint of spice.

❺ nv Chilean Merlot, Santa Lucia, Central Valley, Chile, £2.99, Aldi

This isn't a riproaring Chilean Merlot like the Sainsbury's one above, but it's a very pleasant, typically Chilean mix of plum and blackcurrant fruit, leafy acidity and peppery bite.

❻ 2003 Montepulciano d'Abruzzo, Collezione Italiana, Abruzzo, Italy, £2.79, Aldi

Chunky Italian red at a *very* low price. And it tastes like a good Montepulciano should – solid plum fruit, an earthy undertow and a tweak of black bitterness. A plate of pasta beckons.

❼ nv Badgers Creek Australian Red Wine, South Eastern Australia, £3.29, Aldi

This is an interesting melange of grapes, with Grenache and Petit Verdot on top of the pile, and the result is a pretty tasty drop of typical Aussie grog – plum and loganberry fruit with just a whiff of spice and smoky toast.

❽ 2003 Claret, Bordeaux, France, £2.69, Morrisons

Remarkably, for an area of France that is famous for overpriced, overhyped reds, there's a lot of good cheap Bordeaux around just now. This is the best of them, but you've got to like the style: it's bone dry, relying on a surprisingly happy marriage of soft red strawberry, leafy freshness and chewy earthiness for its effect.

❾ 2003 Chardonnay, Budavár, Danubiana, Hungary, £2.69, Aldi

Very pleasant basic modern Chardonnay. It's not ripe and soft like a New World style Chardonnay, but has attractive white melon fruit and a green leafy acidity balanced by just a hint of sweetness. And at this price, it's a steal.

❿ nv Portuguese Red, JP Vinhos, Portugal,
🍷 £2.99, Sainsbury's
I wish more supermarkets would offer us good basic
Portuguese reds – they have far more character than other
European reds at this price – squashy red fruit sweetened by
strawberry syrup, beefed up with meat and tannin and
churned together in a slightly rogueish way.

> *'squashy red fruit, strawberry syrup, meat*
> *and tannin...slightly rogueish*

⓫ nv Semillon-Chardonnay, Santa Lucia, Mendoza,
♀ Argentina, £2.99, Aldi
This was originally an Aussie blending idea, but the
Argentinians do it quite well. Apple flesh and toffee syrup
richness matched by grapefruit acidity and even some
grapefruit blossom perfume.

⓬ 2003 Colombard-Chardonnay, Petit Herisson, Vin de
♀ Pays des Côtes de Gascogne, France, £2.99, Morrisons
This wine's name translates as 'little hedgehog' – not a
particularly reassuring suggestion – but it's good basic white,
rather stony and dry, but with just enough fresh apple fruit.

Supermarket sparklers

Supermarket own-label Champagnes have had a lot of
attention in the last couple of years, frequently outshining
supposedly glitzier labels. Well it's no fluke. I've done the
tastings too, and there's some fine stuff out there under the
retailers' own labels. Of course, nothing quite as fine as the
fizz from the new soaring star of sparkling wine producers –
England, good old Blighty, with its lovely chalky Sussex and
Kent downland, just perfect for producing great fizz. The soil's
the same as Champagne's, the weather's not that different.
And our lads have got real attitude.

❶ 1996 Première Cuvée, Blanc de Blancs, Chardonnay,
Nyetimber, West Sussex, England, £20.99, Waitrose
Andy Hill was the highly successful songwriter for Bucks Fizz.
Well, now he owns Nyetimber – tucked under the Sussex
Downs, along some of the most impenetrable meandering

For more wine recommendations see Oz Clarke's Wine Style Guide, pages 92–101

lanes you're ever likely to get lost in – where he produces stunning sparkling wine. English sparklers are some of the best in the world – but they're also thrillingly different. Nyetimber soars over your palate and blasts into your brain on the wings of an acidity that would make the mouth of a boulder water with anticipation. It's a supremely self-confident acidity, wrapped in a swirling yeasty cloud of Horlicks and crème fraîche and hazelnuts.

❷ **nv Champagne Blanc de Noirs, Prince William Reserve, Alexandre Bonnet, France, £13.99, Somerfield**
Somerfield's own-label Champagnes have been excellent for years. This one is made by Alexandre Bonnet, who farms some of Champagne's warmest acres in the south of the region – so he gets beautifully ripe grapes just about every year. And especially lovely plump black grapes, which he uses to make this smasher. It has an irresistible mix of apple flavours: half almost overripe loft apples wrapped in paper that you hope will last till Christmas day, half an orchard sweetness like Aspalls Suffolk apple juice. Add some Horlicksy yeast, and you have a Champagne that's both heavyweight and refreshing.

❸ **Sparkling Shiraz, Hardys Crest, Australia, £9.99, Tesco**
Hardys also makes Banrock Station Sparkling Shiraz, but this little number seems to foam a bit more, the lacy fizz that spills over the lip of your glass seems just a little more purple, and the fruit seems that bit sweeter and blacker – black plums and blackberries.

❹ **nv Champagne Premier Cru Brut, Prince William Union Champagne, France, 14.99, Somerfield**
Quite a few high street retailers buy their Champagne from the excellent Union co-operative at Avize – and the results are consistently good. Avize is a top village producing gentle, creamy, foaming wine with good fresh apple fruit and a lingering flavour of oatmeal. Bubbly for the cool dude.

> *'gentle, creamy, foaming...*
> *bubbly for the cool dude*

❺ **nv Champagne Blanc de Noirs, France, £13.99, Tesco**
Black grapes give extra weight to a Champagne – sometimes too much so if the grapes are not expertly grown and carefully pressed. But this one's well done – it *is* weighty, there's good apple and strawberry and a dollop of cream, but it's very nicely balanced too and the weight dissolves on your tongue into something much more light and fanciful.

❻ nv Champagne Blanc de Blancs, Premier Cru, De Saint Gall, Union Champagne, France, £18.99, Marks & Spencer
Classy wine which I would like to see just a little bit older. Yet it works because of the ripe, soft quality of the Chardonnay, mellow fruit, a delightful coiling sparkle and a dancing, tingling acidity that broadens out to a gentle, creamy finish.

❼ nv Champagne, Drappier Carte d'Or, France, £17.99, Co-op
Drappier are serious Champagne makers, so it's nice to see the Co-op bringing them to the high street. This is a good, full-bodied style, with top apple fruit and creamy yeast texture nicely balanced.

❽ nv Century, Chapel Down, Kent, England, £11.99, Sainsbury's
This is a smart cuvée from Chapel Down, who make a larrge and excellent range of wines in the Kentish Weald. What I like about it is that the wine keeps its uniquely English grapefruit and elderflower fruit at the same time as reproducing the creamy and very slightly sweet yet acid texture that is typical of Champagne.

> *'uniquely English grapefruit and elderflower fruit...texture typical of Champagne*

❾ nv Crémant de Bourgogne, Burgundy, France, £8.99, Tesco
Fizz made in Burgundy, a short drive south of Champagne. This one is made from black grapes only – and this could give you a heavy wine, but it doesn't. It's a gentle, biscuity, creamy style shot through with refreshing acidity that is very much like Champagne. So if you want to save a few quid yet still drink high-quality French, try this.

❿ nv Bluff Hill Rosé, New Zealand, £7.99, Marks & Spencer
New Zealand makes some of the New World's best sparkling wine, with a strong resemblance to good Champagne. This is a delightful pink wine, foaming in the glass and showing off loads of fluffy apple peel and strawberry fruit.

⓫ 2001 Cava Brut Vintage, Roca i Amat, Spain, £5.99, Morrisons
Good, full, straight-up Cava with a bit more class than most – apple and pepper, a pinch of earth and some syrupy softness all piled high with foam.

⓬ 1999 Cava Brut Vintage, Spain, £6.99, Somerfield
You don't often get Cava this mature, yet it's retained a fair bit of youth and a lively bubble to go with the quite rich apple and honey fruit and citrus scent.

Fortified & sweet wines

Too many sherries we tasted this year were bland or even baked. This was particularly true of the dry styles. Given that *Hell's Kitchen* is sponsored by Tio Pepe and is still garnering enormous audiences, this seems to be the time to make dry sherries *more* characterful, not less. But then, I'm not a marketing man, so what do I know? At least the quality of ports and sweet wines seems to have improved. Let's be thankful for small mercies.

❶ Muscat de Frontignan, Domaine d'Arain, Languedoc, France, £3.99/500ml, Somerfield [SWEET]
Mmm. Dee-lishous. Fantastic stuff at a fantastic price, the absolute oozing essence of superripe Muscat grapes from down near the Med. If these sweet wines were in fashion, this would be twice the price. But they're not, so it's cheap as chips. And what you get is fat, viscous, gooey wine reeking of sticky grape juice and pineapple chunks crystallized in sugar.

❷ Tawny Port, Aged 10 Years, W & J Graham, Portugal, £10.99, Sainsbury's [SWEET]
Beautiful pure, balanced tawny from the top house of Graham. There's a seductive gentleness about tawny that matches the russet and chestnut colour, a sweetness of date and raisin and nut, a scent like the smell of brown manila envelopes, and just a little nip of spirit to remind you this may cry out to be glugged but if you do, you won't stay on your legs for long.

❸ 1998 Late Bottled Vintage Port, Smith Woodhouse, Portugal, £6.57, ASDA [SWEET]
Fascinating wine, powerful, assertive, not simply a mainstream thick sweet red, like most port is at this price. The smell is heady and swirling with black plums and a smokiness like a flitch of bacon. The taste is richness and power – the spice and black fruit jangling together with peppery spirit into a brawny, cockle-warming cocktail.

❹ 2001 Riesling Eiswein, Ruppertsberger Linsenbusch, Ruppertsberger Winzerverein Hoheburg, Pfalz, Germany, £14.99/half bottle, Sainsbury's [SWEET]
Eiswein is supposed to be a searing struggle between sky-high acidity and dense, ultra-focused fruit. Well, this isn't that. It's rather mellow, well-balanced, gracefully aging. So maybe the Eiswein label is a bit misleading, but the wine is good. It has a typical citrus, petrolly, mature Riesling smell, lots of gently sweet fruit wrapped in custard and pastry and a

fat, lanolin-waxed leather texture. Oh, and just enough grapefruit acidity to get your tongue tingling.

❺ Palo Cortado, Solera Jerezana, Diego Romero, Spain, £6.55, Waitrose [DRY]
Palo Cortado is a strange and rare sherry style – a sweet brown sherry that ended up dry and lean. Well, this is dry-ish, but not palate-cleansingly dry, and the flavour is more like a true Amontillado – off-dry, with a richness of raisins and caramel and buttered brazils.

❻ 2002 Ortega Beerenauslese, Albiger Hundskopf, Ewald Pfeiffer, Rheinhessen, Germany, £6.99/37.5cl, Morrisons [SWEET]
Ortega is one of those strange grapes the Germans invented – literally – to try to produce a Riesling-like wine, but more of it, and riper. Riper certainly, but the flavour has nothing to do with the tense, febrile charms of Riesling. This is a rich, viscous syrup of honeycomb, quince, pineapple chunks and a dash of strawberry, and it's really rather good.

❼ 2000 Maury, Vendange Mise Tardive, Domaine Pouderoux, Roussillon, France, £11.49, Waitrose [SWEET]
Ever wondered what to serve with chocolate? This just might be the wine. It's dark, deep, bittersweet, with blackberries and sloes in syrup, and it has a powerful tannic bite. By itself, it almost hurts. With rough and ready food – or black chocolate – this could be magic.

❽ Fletcher's Fine Ruby Port, Portugal, £4.69, Aldi [SWEET]
Good old Aldi. If you want a gobful of rich, raucous black fruit spiced up with spirit and pepper – look no further. You could even mix it with lemonade.

❾ 2003 Sweet Surrender Pudding Wine, Breede River Valley, Bergsig, Worcester, South Africa, £4.99, Co-op [SWEET]
Chenin Blanc is the main grape here. Since the best thing it does in France is produce sweet wine, it's nice to see the lads in the Cape having a go. This is ripe, with an attractively sharp acidity and full of honeysuckle and sweet apple fruit.

❿ Manzanilla Pale Dry Sherry, Emilio Lustau, Spain, £4.69, Sainsbury's [DRY]
I feel as though this was a very good bone-dry Manzanilla which was then sweetened up: why??? This has really good savoury flavours: bread yeast and a touch of old blue cheese and the dried-up fruit of apples that have been left in the loft *much* too long. And they smooth it out and soften it up!

Storing, serving, tasting

Wine is all about enjoyment, so don't let anyone make you anxious about opening, serving, tasting and storing it. Here are some tips to help you enjoy your wine all the more.

THE CORKSCREW

The first step in tasting any wine is to extract the cork. Look for a corkscrew with an open spiral and a comfortable handle. The Screwpull brand is far and away the best, with a high-quality open spiral. 'Waiter's friend' corkscrews – the type you see used in restaurants – are good too, once you get the knack.

Corkscrews with a solid core that looks like a giant woodscrew tend to mash up delicate corks or get stuck in tough ones. A simple non-levered screw can require a heroic effort. And try to avoid those 'butterfly' corkscrews with the twin lever arms and a bottle opener on the end; they tend to leave cork crumbs floating in the wine.

CORKS

Don't be a cork snob. The only requirements for the seal on a bottle of wine are that it should be hygienic, airtight, long-lasting and removable. Real cork is environmentally friendly, but is prone to shrinkage and infection, which can taint the wine. Synthetic closures modelled on the traditional cork are common in budget wines and are increasingly used by high-quality producers, as are screwcaps, or Stelvin closures.

THE WINE GLASS

The ideal wine glass is a fairly large tulip shape, made of fine, clear glass, with a slender stem. This shape helps to concentrate the aromas of the wine and to show off its colours and texture. For sparkling wine choose a tall, slender glass, as it helps the bubbles to last longer.

Look after your glasses carefully. Detergent residues or grease can affect the flavour of any wine and reduce the bubbliness of sparkling wine. Ideally, wash glasses in very hot water and don't use detergent at all. Rinse glasses thoroughly and allow them to air-dry. Store wine glasses upright to avoid trapping stale odours.

DECANTING

Transferring wine to a decanter brings it into contact with oxygen, which can open up the flavours. You don't need to do it ages before serving and you don't need a special decanter: a glass jug is just as good. And there's no reason why you shouldn't decant the wine to aerate it, then pour it back into its bottle to serve it.

Mature red wine is likely to contain sediment and needs careful handling. Stand the bottle upright for a day or two to let the sediment fall to the bottom. Open the wine carefully, and place a torch or candle beside the decanter. As you pour, stand so that you can see the light shining through the neck of the bottle. Pour the wine into the decanter in one steady

RIEDEL

THE WINE GLASS COMPANY

SOMMELIERS BORDEAUX GRAND CRU

ONLY A RIEDEL GLASS DELIVERS
THE FULL SENSUALITY OF WINE.

motion and stop when you see the sediment reaching the neck of the bottle.

TEMPERATURE

The temperature of wine has a bearing on its flavour. Heavy reds are happy at room temperature, but the lighter the wine the cooler it should be. Juicy, fruity young reds, such as wines from the Loire Valley, are refreshing served lightly chilled; I'd serve Burgundy and other Pinot Noir reds at cool larder temperature.

Chilling white wines makes them taste fresher, but also subdues flavours, so bear this in mind if you're splashing out on a top-quality white – don't keep it in the fridge too long. Sparkling wines, however, *must* be well chilled to avoid exploding corks and fountains of foam.

For quick chilling, fill a bucket with ice and cold water, plus a few spoonfuls of salt if you're in a real hurry. This is much more effective than a fridge or ice on its own. If the wine is already cool a vacuum-walled cooler is ideal for maintaining the temperature.

KEEPING LEFTOVERS

Exposure to oxygen causes wine to deteriorate. It lasts fairly well if you just push the cork back in and stick the bottle in the fridge, but you can also buy a range of effective devices to help keep oxygen at bay. Vacuvin uses a rubber stopper and a vacuum pump to remove air from the bottle. Others inject inert gas into the bottle to shield the wine from the ravages of oxidation.

WINE STORAGE

The longer you keep a bottle of wine, the more important it is to store it with care. If you've got a cellar, lucky you. If not, look around for a nook – under the stairs, a built-in cupboard or a disused fireplace – that is cool, relatively dark and vibration-free, in which you can store the bottles on their sides to keep the corks moist (if a cork dries out it will let air in and spoil the wine).

Wine should be kept in a cool place – around 10–15°C/50–55°F – well away from central heating. It is even more important to avoid sudden temperature changes or extremes: a windowless garage or outhouse

may be cool in summer but may freeze in winter. Exposure to light can very quickly ruin wine, but dark bottles go some way to protecting it from light.

TASTING

On the next page, I'll talk you through the tasting process, but tasting doesn't have to be done in silent, science-lab conditions – it should be fun! Several organizations – and many wine retailers – offer tutored tastings, giving you a chance to compare flavours and discover more about the sort of wines you like.

Visiting wineries is another great way to discover more about wine. English wine is getting better and better, and sometimes the only way to buy it is direct from the vineyard. There are some 350 vineyards in England and Wales, many of which welcome visitors – for details, check out the website www.englishwineproducers.com

Tasting wine in the place it's made is, for many wine lovers, part of the pleasure of a holiday in France, Italy or Spain – and now also in California, Australia, New Zealand and South Africa.

OZ CLARKE
connoisseur range

Electric Corkscrew   Wine Chiller   Ice Shaver   Drinks Maker

Entertain in style with the new Connoisseur Range from Oz Clarke. The range features four smart products that don't just look great, but will impress your party guests time after time. Mix exotic cocktails with the Drinks Maker and use the Ice Shaver for frozen drinks; the Wine Chiller and Electric Corkscrew will ensure your wine is always perfectly served.

All products are available from Argos and John Lewis

How to taste wine

If you just knock your wine back like a cold beer, you'll be missing most of whatever flavour it has to offer. Take a bit of time to pay attention to what you're tasting and I guarantee you'll enjoy the wine more.

Read the label

There's no law that says you have to make life hard for yourself when tasting wine. So have a look at what you're drinking and read the notes on the back label if there is one. The label will tell you the vintage, the region and/or the grape variety, the producer and the alcohol level.

Look at the wine

Pour the wine into a glass so it is a third full and tilt it against a white background so you can enjoy the range of colours in the wine. Is it dark or light? Is it viscous or watery? As you gain experience the look of the wine will tell you one or two things about the age and the likely flavour and weight of the wine. As a wine ages, whites lose their springtime greenness and gather deeper, golden hues, whereas red wines trade the purple of youth for a paler brick red.

Swirl and sniff

Give the glass a vigorous swirl to wake up the aromas in the wine, stick your nose in and inhale gently. This is where you'll be hit by the amazing range of smells a wine can produce. Interpret them in any way that means something to you personally: it's only by reacting honestly to the taste and smell of a wine that you can build up a memory bank of flavours against which to judge future wines.

Take a sip

At last! It's time to drink the wine. So take a decent-sized slurp – enough to fill your mouth about a third full. The tongue can detect only very basic flavour elements: sweetness at the tip, acidity at the sides and bitterness at the back. The real business of tasting goes on in a cavity at the back of the mouth which is really part of the nose. The idea is to get the fumes from the wine to rise up into this nasal cavity. Note the toughness, acidity and sweetness of the wine, then suck some air through the wine to help the flavours on their way. Gently 'chew' the wine and let it coat your tongue, teeth, cheeks and gums. Jot down a few notes as you form your opinion and then make the final decision... Do you like it or don't you?

Swallow or spit it out

If you are tasting a lot of wines, you will have to spit as you go if you want to remain upright and retain your judgement. Otherwise, go ahead and swallow and enjoy the lovely aftertaste of the wine.

WINE FAULTS

If you order wine in a restaurant and you find one of these faults you are entitled to a replacement. Many retailers will also replace a faulty bottle if you return it the day after you open it, with your receipt. Sometimes faults affect random bottles, others may ruin a whole case of wine.

- Cork taint – a horrible musty, mouldy smell indicates 'corked' wine, caused by a contaminated cork
- Volatile acidity – pronounced vinegary or acetone smells
- Oxidation – sherry-like smells are not appropriate in red and white wines
- Hydrogen sulphide – 'rotten eggs' smell.

WATCHPOINTS

- Sediment in red wines makes for a gritty, woody mouthful. To avoid this, either decant the wine or simply pour it gently, leaving the last few centilitres of wine in the bottle.
- White crystals, or tartrates, on the cork or at the bottom of bottles of white wine are both harmless and flavourless.
- Sticky bottle neck – if wine has seeped past the cork it probably hasn't been very well kept and air might have got in. This may mean oxidized wine.
- Excess sulphur dioxide is sometimes noticeable as a smell of a recently struck match; it should dissipate after a few minutes.

Wine style guide

When faced with a shelf – or a screen – packed with different wines from around the world, where do you start? Well, if you're after a particular flavour of wine, my guide to wine styles will point you in the right direction.

RED WINES
Juicy, fruity reds
The definitive modern style for easygoing reds. Tasty, refreshing and delicious with or without food, they pack in loads of crunchy fruit while minimizing the tough, gum-drying tannins that characterize most traditional red wine styles. Beaujolais (made from the Gamay grape) is the prototype, and Loire reds such as Chinon and Saumur (made from Cabernet Franc) pack in the fresh raspberries. Italy's Bardolino, from the Veneto, is light and refreshing. Nowadays, hi-tech producers all over the world are working the magic with a whole host of grape varieties. Carmenère, Merlot and Malbec are always good bets, and Grenache/Garnacha and Tempranillo usually come up with the goods. Italian grapes like Bonarda, Barbera and Sangiovese seem to double in succulence under Argentina's blazing sun. And at around £5 even Cabernet Sauvignon – if it's from somewhere warm like Australia, South America, South Africa or Spain – or a vin de pays Syrah from southern France, will emphasize the fruit and hold back on the tannin.

- 2003 Garnacha, Vineyard X, Campo de Borja, Bodegas Borsao, Aragón, Spain, £3.99, Thresher
- 2004 Bonarda-Sangiovese, Santa Julia, Familia Zuccardi, Mendoza, Argentina, £4.99, Morrisons, Waitrose
- 2003 Grenache, Peter Lehmann, Barossa, Australia, £5.99, Flagship Wines, Morrisons, Oddbins, Tesco, Unwins, Vin du Vin
- 2003 Bourgueil, La Coudraye, Yannick Amirault, Loire Valley, France, £6.75, Lea and Sandeman
- 2004 Beaujolais, Jean-François Garlon, France, £7.05, Roger Harris

Silky, strawberryish reds
Here we're looking for some special qualities, specifically a gorgeously smooth texture and a heavenly fragrance of strawberries, raspberries or cherries. We're looking for soft, decadent, seductive wines. One grape – Pinot Noir – and one region –

bottled
passion

where else can you get passion for only £4.99?

Produced by the award winning Familia Zuccardi
ARGENTINA

AUVIGNON BLANC · VIOGNIER · CHARDONNAY · BONARDA SANGIOVESE · TEMPRANILLO
SYRAH ROSÉ · PINOT NOIR · MERLOT · MALBEC · CABERNET SAUVIGNON

UK Agent
01794 507100
info@thierrys.co.uk

www.familiazuccardi.com

Burgundy – stand out and prices are high to astronomical. Good red Burgundy is addictively hedonistic and all sorts of strange decaying aromas start to hover around the strawberries as the wine ages. Pinot Noirs from New Zealand, California, Oregon and, increasingly, Australia come close, but they're expensive, too; Chilean Pinots are far more affordable. You can get that strawberry perfume (though not the silky texture) from other grapes in Spain's Navarra or Rioja and up-coming regions like La Mancha and Murcia. Southern Rhône blends can deliver if you look for fairly light examples of Côtes du Rhône-Villages or Costières de Nîmes.

- 2003 Lacrima di Morro d'Alba, Rubico, Marotti Campi, Marche, Italy, £7.99, Oddbins
- 2001 Rioja Crianza, Conde de Valdemar, Spain, £8.29, Oddbins
- 2004 Pinot Noir, Las Brisas Vineyard, Viña Leyda, Leyda, Chile, £8.99 Co-op, £10.59 Adnams
- 2002 Mercurey, Château de Chamirey, Burgundy, France, £14.25, Jeroboams
- 2002 Pinot Noir, Carrick, Cairnmuir Road Winery, Central Otago, New Zealand, £19.95, Great Western Wine

Intense, blackcurranty reds

Firm, intense wines which often only reveal their softer side with a bit of age; Cabernet Sauvignon is the grape, on its own or blended with Merlot or other varieties. Bordeaux is the classic region but there are far too many overpriced underachievers there. And Cabernet's image has changed. You can still choose the austere, tannic style, in theory aging to a heavenly cassis and cedar maturity, but most of the world is taking a fruitier blackcurrant-and-mint approach. Chile does the fruity style par excellence. New Zealand can deliver Bordeaux-like flavours, but in a faster-maturing wine. Australia often adds a medicinal eucalyptus twist or a dollop of blackcurrant jam. Argentina and South Africa are making their mark too.

- 2000 Cabernet Sauvignon, Nativa, Carmen, Maipo Valley, Chile, £7.99, Butlers Wine Cellar, Waitrose, Wright Wine Co
- 2002 Cabernet Sauvignon, Springfield Estate, Robertson, South Africa, £8.99, Booths
- 2001 Cabernet Sauvignon, Chapel Hill, McLaren Vale/ Coonawarra, South Australia, £9.99, Tesco
- 2002 Cabernet Sauvignon-Merlot, Villa Maria Reserve, Hawkes Bay, New Zealand, £14.99, Wimbledon Wine Cellar
- 2001 Cheval des Andes, Mendoza, Argentina, £45, Harrods (tel: 020 7730 1234), Wimbledon Wine Cellar

Spicy, warm-hearted reds

Australian Shiraz is the epitome of this rumbustious, riproaring style: dense, rich, chocolaty, sometimes with a twist of pepper, a whiff of smoke, or a slap of leather. But it's not alone. There are southern Italy's Primitivo and Nero d'Avola, California's Zinfandel, Mexico's Petite Sirah, Argentina's Malbec, South Africa's Pinotage, Toro from Spain and some magnificent Greek reds. In southern France the wines of the Languedoc often show this kind of warmth, roughed up with hillside herbs. And if you want your spice more serious, more smoky and minerally, go for the classic wines of the northern Rhône Valley.

- 2002 Petite Sirah, L A Cetto, Mexico, £5.35, Waitrose
- 2003 Syrah, Porcupine Ridge, Boekenhoutskloof, South Africa, £6.99, Waitrose
- 2003 Nero d'Avola-Syrah, Benuara, Cusumano, Sicily, Italy, £8.49, Oddbins
- 2003 Rasteau, Cuvée Prestige, Domaine des Coteaux des Travers, Rhône Valley, France, £8.99, Booths
- 2002 Shiraz-Cabernet Sauvignon, Pondalowie Vineyards, Central Victoria, Australia, £12.99, Australian Wine Club

Mouthwatering, sweet-sour reds

Sounds weird? This style is the preserve of Italy, and it's all about food: the rasp of sourness cuts through rich, meaty food, with a lip-smacking tingle that works equally well with pizza or tomato-based pasta dishes. But there's fruit in there too – cherries and plums – plus raisiny sweetness and a herby bite. The wines are now better made than ever, with more seductive fruit, but holding on to those fascinating flavours. You'll have to shell out up to a tenner for decent Chianti; more for Piedmont wines (especially Barolo and Barbaresco, so try Langhe instead). Valpolicella can be very good, but choose with care. Portugal can deliver something of the same character with its sour-cherries reds. Oddball grapes like Chambourcin often have these flavours.

- 2003 Brindisi Rosso, Cantine Due Palme, Puglia, Italy, £5.99, Sainsbury's
- 2003 Shiraz-Sangiovese Il Briccone, Primo Estate, South Australia, £9.99, Australian Wine Club
- 2000 Quinta do Passadouro Vinho Tinto, Douro, Portugal, £12.99, D Byrne, Flying Corkscrew
- 2001 Amarone della Valpolicella Classico, Vignale, Veneto, Italy, £13.99, Waitrose
- 2000 Brunello di Montalcino, Tenuta Nuova, Casanova de Neri, Tuscany, Italy, £20, Waitrose

Delicate (and not-so-delicate) rosé

Dry rosé can be wonderful, with flavours of strawberries and maybe herbs. Look for wines made from sturdy grapes like Cabernet, Syrah or Merlot, or go for Grenache/Garnacha or Tempranillo from Spain and the Rhône Valley. South America is a good, flavoursome bet for this style of wine.

- **2004 Valdepeñas Rosado, Viña Albali,** Castilla-La Mancha, Spain, £4.69, Unwins
- **2005 Syrah Rosé, Santa Julia,** Familia Zuccardi, Mendoza, Argentina, £4.99, Somerfield, Thresher
- **2004 Costières de Nîmes Rosé, Château Guiot,** Rhône Valley, France, £5.29, Majestic Wine
- **2004 Cabernet Sauvignon Rosé, Santa Rita,** Maipo Valley, Chile, c.£6, Majestic Wine, Sainsbury's
- **2004 Rosato, Castello di Ama,** IGT Toscana, Tuscany, Italy, £8.04, John Armit

WHITE WINES
Bone-dry, neutral whites

Neutral wines exist for the sake of seafood or to avoid interrupting you while you're eating. It's a question of balance, rather than aromas and flavours, but there will be a bit of lemon, yeast and a mineral thrill in a good Muscadet sur lie or a proper Chablis. Loads of Italian whites do the same thing, but Italy is increasingly picking up on the global shift towards fruit flavours and maybe some oak. Basic, cheap South African whites are often a good bet if you want something thirst-quenching and easy to drink. Colombard and Chenin are fairly neutral grape varieties widely used in South Africa, often producing appley flavours, and better examples add a lick of honey.

- **2004 Viña Sol, Torres,** Cataluña, Spain, £4.68, ASDA
- **2004 Muscadet Côtes de Grandlieu sur lie, Fief Guérin,** Loire Valley, France, £4.99, Waitrose
- **2004 Chenin Blanc, Peter Lehmann,** Barossa Valley, South Australia, c.£5, Budgens, Co-op, Waitrose
- **2004 Lugana, Villa Flora, Zenato,** Veneto, Italy, £5.99, Waitrose
- **2000 Ktima Papagiannakos,** Attica, Greece, £6.60, Savage Selection

Green, tangy whites

For nerve-tingling refreshment, Sauvignon Blanc is the classic grape, full of fresh grass, gooseberry and nettle flavours. I always used to go for New Zealand versions, but I'm now more inclined to reach for an inexpensive bottle from Chile, South Africa or Hungary. Or even a simple white Bordeaux, because suddenly Bordeaux Sauvignon is buzzing with life. Most Sancerre and the other Loire Sauvignons are overpriced. Austria's Grüner Veltliner has a peppery freshness. Alternatively, look at Riesling. Australia serves it up with bountiful lime and toast flavours while classic German versions are steelier and green-apple fresh, with intriguing peach and smoke flavours in their youth.

- **2004 Vin de Pays des Côtes de Gascogne, Domaine de Pellehaut,** South-West France, £3.99, Booths
- **2004 Vinho Verde, Quinta de Simaens,** Portugal, £5.49, Waitrose
- **2005 Riesling, Tim Adams,** Clare Valley, South Australia, £7.99, Tesco
- **2004 Sauvignon Blanc, Life from Stone, Springfield Estate,** Robertson, South Africa, £7.99, Booths
- **2004 Sauvignon Blanc, Jackson Estate,** Marlborough, New Zealand, £8.50–10, Booths, Majestic, Oddbins, Wright Wine Co

Intense, nutty whites

The best white Burgundy from the Côte d'Or cannot be bettered for its combination of soft nut and oatmeal flavours, subtle, buttery oak and firm, dry structure. Prices are often hair-raising and the cheaper wines rarely offer much Burgundy style. For £6 or £7 your best bet is oaked Chardonnay from an innovative Spanish region such as Somontano or Navarra. You'll get a nutty, creamy taste and nectarine fruit with good oak-aged white Bordeaux or traditional white Rioja. Top Chardonnays from New World countries – and Italy for that matter – can emulate Burgundy, but once again we're looking at serious prices.

- **2003 Rioja, Torresoto,** Companía Vinícola del Norte de Espana, Spain, £4.99, Marks & Spencer
- **2003 Mâcon-Chardonnay, White Burgundy, Cuvée Paul Talmard,** Burgundy, France, £6.99, Adnams
- **2002 Chardonnay, Winemaker's Lot, Concha y Toro,** Casablanca, Chile, £7.99, Virgin Wines
- **2004 Sauvignon Blanc-Semillon, Cape Mentelle,** Western Australia, £10.99, Waitrose
- **2003 Bourgogne Blanc, Domaine de Montmeix,** Domaine Borgeot, Burgundy, France, £11.99, Oddbins

Ripe, toasty whites

Aussie Chardonnay conquered the world with its upfront flavours of peaches, apricots and melons, usually spiced up by the vanilla, toast and butterscotch richness of new oak. This winning style has now become a standard-issue flavour produced by all sorts of countries, though I still love the original. You don't need to spend more than a fiver for a great big friendly wine, though a well-spent £8 or so will give you more to relish beyond the second glass. Oaked Australian Semillon can also give rich, ripe fruit flavours. If you see the words 'unoaked' or 'cool-climate' on an Aussie bottle, expect an altogether leaner drink.

- **2003 Semillon, Peter Lehmann,** Barossa Valley, South Australia, c.£6, widely available
- **2004 Chardonnay-Viognier-Marsanne, Novas,** Casablanca Valley, Chile, £7.95, Vintage Roots
- **2004 Chardonnay The Olive Grove, D'Arenberg,** McLaren Vale, South Australia, £7.99, Oddbins
- **2003 Semillon, Steenberg,** Constantia, South Africa, £7.99 Booths, £9 John Armit
- **2003 Chardonnay, Warwick Estate,** Stellenbosch, South Africa, £8.99, Waitrose

Aromatic whites

Alsace has always been a plentiful source of perfumed, dry or off-dry whites: Gewürztraminer with its rose and lychee scent or Muscat with its floral, hothouse grape perfume. A few producers in New Zealand, Australia, Chile and South Africa are having some success with these grapes. Floral, apricotty Viognier, traditionally the grape of Condrieu in the northern Rhône, now appears in vins de pays from all over southern France and also from California and Australia. Condrieu is expensive (£20 will get you entry-level stuff and no guarantee that it will be fragrant); vin de pays wines start at around £5 and are just as patchy. Albariño from Rías Baixas in Spain is more reliable. For aroma on a budget grab some Hungarian Irsai Oliver or Argentinian Torrontes.

- **2004 Viognier, Domaine de la Bastide,** Vin de Pays d'Hauterive, Languedoc, France, £4.99, Booths
- **2004 Torrontes, Crios de Susana Balbo, Dominio del Plata,** Cafayate, Argentina, £5.49, Anthony Byrne
- **2003 Alsace Gewurztraminer,** Kuehn, £6.99, Tesco Finest

- 2004 Gewurztraminer, Winemaker's Lot, Concha y Toro, Chile, £7.49, Oddbins
- 2004 Gewurztraminer, Villa Maria Private Bin, New Zealand, c.£8, ASDA, Majestic Wine, Waitrose

Golden, sweet whites

Good sweet wines are difficult to make and therefore expensive: prices for Sauternes and Barsac (from Bordeaux) can go through the roof, but near-neighbours Monbazillac, Loupiac, Saussignac and Ste-Croix-du-Mont are more affordable. Sweet Loire wines such as Quarts de Chaume, Bonnezeaux and some Vouvrays have a quince aroma and a fresh acidity that can keep them lively for decades, as do sweet Rieslings, such as Alsace Vendange Tardive, German and Austrian Beerenauslese (BA), Trockenbeerenauslese (TBA) and Eiswein. Canadian icewine is quite rare over here, but we're seeing more of Hungary's Tokaji, with its sweet-sour, marmalade flavours.

- 2003 La Beryl Blanc, Fairview, South Africa, £9.25/50 cl, Butlers Wine Cellar
- 2002 Saussignac, Cuvée Flavie, Château des Eyssards, South-West France, £11.73/50 cl, Flagship Wines
- 1997 Scheurebe Eiswein, Ungsteiner Hönigsäckel, Darting Estate, Pfalz, Germany, £12/37.5 cl, Marks & Spencer
- 2000 De Bortoli Noble One Botrytis Semillon, NSW, Australia, £13–14/37.5 cl, O W Loeb, Majestic, Noble Rot, Wright Wine Co
- 2003 Coteaux du Layon, Clos de Sainte Catherine, Domaine des Baumard, Loire Valley, France, £21.25, Jeroboams

SPARKLING WINES

Champagne can be the finest sparkling wine on the planet, but fizz made by the traditional Champagne method in Australia, New Zealand or California – often using the same grape varieties – is often just as good and cheaper. It might be a little more fruity, where Champagne concentrates on bready, yeasty or nutty

Wine style guide

CHAMPAGNE
BILLECART-SALMON
Maison Fondée en 1818

www.champagne-billecart.fr

aromas, but a few are dead ringers for the classic style. Fizz is also made in other parts of France: Crémant de Bourgogne is one of the best. England is beginning to show its potential. Spain's Cava is perfect party fizz available at bargain basement prices in all the big supermarkets.

- NV Jansz, Australia, £10–11, Noble Rot, Oddbins, Selfridges
- NV Pelorus, Cloudy Bay, Marlborough, New Zealand, c.£12.50–14, Booths, Connolly's, Wright Wine
- 1996 Blanc de Blancs, Nyetimber, England, c.£21, Ballantynes, Berry Bros & Rudd, Waitrose, Wright Wine, Noel Young
- NV Champagne Brut Réserve, Billecart-Salmon, £23–25, Berry Bros & Rudd, Fortnum & Mason, Halifax Wine Co, Harvey Nichols, Lay & Wheeler, James Nicholson, Oddbins, Playford Ros
- NV Champagne 'R' de Ruinart Brut, France, c.£28, Fortnum & Mason, S H Jones, Lea and Sandeman, Philglas & Swiggot, Playford Ros

---

How to buy vegetarian and vegan wine

Virtually all wine is clarified with 'fining' agents, many of which are animal by-products. Although they are not present in the finished wine, they are clearly not acceptable for strict vegetarians and vegans. Non-animal alternatives such as bentonite clay are widely used and vegan wines rely solely on these; vegetarian wines can use egg whites or milk proteins.

• **Specialist merchants** Organic specialists such as Vinceremos and Vintage Roots assess every wine on their lists for its vegetarian or vegan status.

• **Supermarkets** Most supermarkets stock some vegetarian and vegan wines and identify own-label ones with a symbol, such as the 'V' logo used by Somerfield and Marks & Spencer.

• **Other outlets** Check the labels. Some producers, such as Chapoutier, use a 'V' symbol to indicate vegetarian wines.

FORTIFIED WINES
Tangy, appetizing fortified wines

To set your taste buds tingling, fino and manzanilla sherries are pale, perfumed, bone-dry and bracingly tangy. True amontillado, dark and nutty, is also dry. Dry oloroso adds deep, raisiny flavours. Palo cortado falls somewhere between amontillado and oloroso, and manzanilla pasada is an older, nuttier style of manzanilla.

The driest style of Madeira, Sercial, is steely and smoky; Verdelho Madeira is a bit fuller and richer, but still tangy and dry.

- **Manzanilla Mariscal**, Dolores Bustillo Delgado, £6.70, Tanners
- **Fino Inocente**, Valdespino, £9.60, Wright Wine, Noel Young
- **Amontillado Del Duque**, González Byass, c.£11–12/half bottle, Sainsbury's, Villeneuve Wines
- **Oloroso Solera 1842**, Valdespino, £11.99/half bottle, Waitrose
- **10 Year Old Sercial Madeira**, Henriques & Henriques, £16.99/50 cl, Majestic, Waitrose, Tanners, Noel Young Wines

Rich, warming fortified wines

Raisins and brown sugar, dried figs and caramelized nuts – do you like the sound of that? Port is the classic dark sweet wine, and it comes in several styles, from basic ruby, to tawny, matured in cask for 10 years or more, to vintage, which matures to mellowness in the bottle. The Portuguese island of Madeira produces fortified wines with rich brown smoky flavours and a startling bite of acidity: the sweet styles to look for are Bual and Malmsey. Decent sweet sherries are rare; oloroso dulce is a style with stunningly concentrated flavours. In southern France, Banyuls and Maury are deeply fruity fortified wines. Marsala, from Sicily, has rich brown sugar flavours with a refreshing sliver of acidity. The versatile Muscat grape makes luscious golden wines all around the Mediterranean, but also pops up in orange, black, and the gloriously rich, treacly brown versions that Australia does superbly.

- **Muscat de Frontignan, Domaine d'Arain**, Languedoc, France, £3.99/50 cl, Somerfield
- **Montilla, Gran Barquero PX**, Spain, £6.49/50 cl, Waitrose
- **Noé Very Old Pedro Ximénez**, González Byass, Spain, £11–12/half bottle, Tesco, Villeneuve Wines
- **1999 Crusted Port, Graham's**, Portugal, c.£14, Thresher
- **15 Year Old Malmsey Madeira**, Henriques & Henriques, £16.49/50 cl, Tanners, Waitrose, Noel Young Wines
- **Rutherglen Grand Muscat**, Chambers Rosewood Vineyards, Victoria, Australia, £21.95/half bottle, Lay & Wheeler

Buying for the long term

Most of this book is about wines to drink more or less immediately – that's how modern wines are made, and that's what you'll find in most high street retail outlets. If you're looking for a mature vintage of a great wine that's ready to drink – or are prepared to wait 10 years or more for a great vintage to reach its peak – specialist wine merchants will be able to help; the internet's another good place to look for mature wines. Here's my beginners' guide to buying wine at auction and *en primeur*.

AUCTIONS

A wine sale catalogue from one of the UK's auction houses will have wine enthusiasts drooling over names they certainly don't see every day. Better still, the lots are often of mature vintages that are ready to drink. Before you go, find out all you can about the producer and vintages described in the catalogue. My *Pocket Wine Book* is a good place to start, or Michael Broadbent's *Vintage Wines* for old and rare wines, and the national wine magazines (*Decanter*, *Wine International*) run regular features on wine regions and their vintages. You can also learn a lot from tutored tastings – especially 'vertical' tastings, which compare different vintages. This is important – some merchants take the opportunity to clear inferior vintages at auction.

The drawbacks? You have no guarantee that the wine has been well stored, and if it's faulty you have little chance of redress. But for expensive and mature wines, I have to say that the top auction houses nowadays make a considerable effort to check the provenance and integrity of the wines. As prices of the most sought-after wines have soared, so it has become profitable either to forge the bottles and their contents or to try to pass off stock that is clearly out of condition. And don't forget that there will often be a commission, or buyers premium, to pay, so check out the small print in the sale catalogue. Online wine auctions have similar pros and cons.

If you've never bought wine at an auction before, a good place to start would be a local auctioneers such as Straker Chadwick in Abergavenny (tel: 01873 852624, www.strakerchadwick.co.uk) or Morphets in Harrogate (01423 530030, www.morphets.co.uk); they're less intimidating than the famous London houses of Christie's and Sotheby's and you may come away with some really exciting wine.

BUYING EN PRIMEUR

En primeur is a French term for wine which is sold before it is bottled, sometimes referred to as a 'future'. In the spring after the vintage the Bordeaux châteaux – and a few other wine-producing regions – hold tastings of barrel samples for members of the international wine trade. The châteaux then offer a proportion of their production to the wine merchants (négociants) in Bordeaux, who in turn offer it to wine merchants around the world at an opening price. The advantage to the châteaux is that their capital is not tied up in expensive stock for the next year or two, until the wines are bottled and ready to ship.

Traditionally merchants would buy en primeur for stock to be sold later at a higher price, while offering their customers the chance to take advantage of the opening prices as well. The idea of private individuals investing rather than institutions took off with a series of good Bordeaux vintages in the 1980s.

WINE FOR THE FUTURE

There is a lot to be said for buying en primeur. For one thing, in a great vintage you may be able to find the finest and rarest wines far more cheaply than they will ever appear again. This was especially true of the 1990 vintage in Bordeaux; this, in turn, primed the market for the exceptional vintages of 1999 in Burgundy and 2000 in Bordeaux. Equally, when a wine – even a relatively inexpensive one – is made in very limited quantities, buying en primeur may be practically your only chance of getting hold of it.

In the past, British wine merchants and their privileged customers were able to 'buy double what you want, sell half for double what you paid, and

drink for free', but as the market has opened up to people more interested in making a quick buck than drinking fine wine, the whole process has become more risky.

Another potential hazard is that a tasting assessment is difficult at an early date. There is a well-founded suspicion that many barrel samples are doctored (legally) to appeal to the most powerful consumer critics, in particular the American Robert Parker and the *Wine Spectator* magazine. The wine that is finally bottled may or may not bear a resemblance to what was tasted in the spring following the vintage. In any case, most serious red wines are in a difficult stage of their evolution in the spring, and with the best will in the world it is possible to get one's

CLARKE'S CANNY PICKS

In the spring of 2005 I went to Bordeaux and tasted hundreds of young wines from the 2004 vintage. I've narrowed my notes down to a dozen of my favourites – all delicious and fairly priced wines – to buy en primeur, for drinking, not selling on.

- ✪ Château Branaire-Ducru (St-Julien)
- ✪ Château Cap de Mourlin (St-Émilion Grand Cru)
- ✪ Clos Fourtet (St-Émilion Premier Grand Cru Classé)
- ✪ Château Cos Labory (St-Estèphe)
- ✪ Château Ferrière (Margaux)
- ✪ Château Haut-Bages Libéral (Pauillac)
- ✪ Château Léoville-Barton (St-Julien)
- ✪ Château Malescot St-Exupéry (Margaux)
- ✪ Château Monbrison (Margaux)
- ✪ Château Les Ormes de Pez (St-Estèphe)
- ✪ Château Poujeaux (Moulis)
- ✪ Château du Tertre (Margaux)

evaluation wrong. However, the aforementioned Americans, and magazines like *Decanter* and *Wine International*, will do their best to offer you accurate judgements on the newly offered wines, and most merchants who make a *primeur* offer also write a good assessment of the wines. You will find that many of them quote the Parker or *Wine Spectator* marks. Anything over 90 out of 100 risks being hyped and hiked in price. Many of the best bargains get marks between 85 and 89, since the 90+ marks are generally awarded for power rather than subtlety. Consideration can be given to the producer's reputation for consistency and to the general vintage assessment for the region.

Prices can go down as well as up. They may easily not increase significantly in the few years after the campaign.

Some popular vintages are offered at ridiculously high prices – some unpopular ones too. It's only about twice a decade that the combination of high quality and fair prices offers the private buyer a chance of a good, guaranteed profit. Interestingly, if one highly touted vintage is followed by another, the prices for the second one often have to fall because the market simply will not accept two inflated price structures in a row. Recent Bordeaux examples of this are the excellent 1990 after the much hyped 1989 and the potentially fine 2001 after the understandably hyped 2000.

2003 was hot and dry in Bordeaux: the heavier, less classic – but more water-retentive – clay soils of the Médoc made many of the best wines, at reasonable prices. Well-known Médoc wines as well as St-Émilions and Pomerols are more patchy in quality in 2003 – but it is already too late to invest in 2003 for profit. 2004 was a bigger, more classic, but more erratic vintage in Bordeaux; the good news is that prices dropped by a third, so it's not a bad time to dip your toe into the future.

SECURE CELLARAGE

Another worry is that the merchant you buy the wine from may not still be around to deliver it to you two years later. Buy from a merchant you trust, with a solid trading base in other wines.

Once the wines are shipped you may want your merchant to store the wine for you; there is usually a small charge for this. If your merchant offers cellarage, you should insist that (1) you receive a stock certificate; (2) your wines are stored separately from the merchant's own stocks; and (3) your cases are identifiable as your property and are labelled accordingly. All good merchants offer these safeguards as a minimum service.

CHECK THE SMALL PRINT

Traditional wine merchants may quote prices exclusive of VAT and/or duty: wine may not be the bargain it first appears.

A wine quoted *en primeur* is usually offered on an ex-cellars (EC) basis; the price excludes shipping, duties and taxes such as VAT. A price quoted in bond (IB) in the UK includes shipping, but excludes duties and taxes. Duty paid (DP) prices exclude VAT. You should check beforehand the exact terms of sale with your merchant, who will give you a projection of the final 'duty paid delivered' price.

SPECIALIST MERCHANTS OFFERING 'EN PRIMEUR'

Full details for these merchants can be found in our retailers directory, starting on page 106

- ✪ Adnams, John Armit, Averys
- ✪ Ballantynes, H & H Bancroft, Bennetts, Berry Bros & Rudd, Bibendum, Bordeaux Index, Butlers Wine Cellar, Anthony Byrne, D Byrne
- ✪ Cave Cru Classé, ChâteauOnline, Cockburns of Leith, Connolly's, Corney & Barrow
- ✪ Direct Wine Shipments, Domaine Direct
- ✪ Farr Vintners, Fortnum & Mason, Friarwood
- ✪ Gauntleys, Goedhuis, Great Western Wine
- ✪ Haynes Hanson & Clark, Hedley Wright, Hicks & Don
- ✪ Jeroboams, S H Jones, Justerini & Brooks
- ✪ Laithwaites, Lay & Wheeler, Lea & Sandeman, O W Loeb
- ✪ Mayfair Cellars, Millésima, Montrachet
- ✪ James Nicholson, Nickolls & Perks
- ✪ Christopher Piper, Playford Ros, Portland Wine
- ✪ Raeburn Fine Wines, Howard Ripley, Roberson
- ✪ Savage Selection, Seckford Wines
- ✪ Tanners
- ✪ Wimbledon Wine Cellar, The Wine Society, Peter Wylie
- ✪ Noel Young Wines

Retailers directory

All these retailers have been chosen on the basis of the quality and interest of their lists. If you want to find local suppliers, retailers are listed by region in the Who's Where directory on page 144.

The following services are available where indicated:
C = cellarage **G** = glass hire/loan
M = mail order **T** = tastings and talks

A & B Vintners

Little Tawsden, Spout Lane, Brenchley, Kent TN12 7AS (01892) 724977 FAX (01892) 722673 E-MAIL info@abvintners.co.uk WEBSITE www.abvintners.co.uk HOURS Mon–Fri 9–6 CARDS MasterCard, Visa DELIVERY Free 5 cases or more, otherwise £11.75 per consignment UK mainland MINIMUM ORDER 1 mixed case EN PRIMEUR Bandol, Burgundy, Languedoc, Rhône. **C M T**
✪ **Star attractions** *Impressive list with a string of top-quality domaines from Burgundy and the Rhône, and little-known gems from the Languedoc and Bandol.*

Adnams

HEAD OFFICE & MAIL ORDER
Sole Bay Brewery, Southwold, Suffolk IP18 6JW (01502) 727222 FAX (01502) 727223 E-MAIL wines@adnams.co.uk WEBSITE www.adnamswines.co.uk SHOPS The Wine Cellar & Kitchen Store, Victoria Street, Southwold, Suffolk IP18 6JW • The Wine Shop, Pinkney's Lane, Southwold, Suffolk IP18 6EW HOURS (Orderline) Mon–Fri 9–8, Sat 9–5; Wine Cellar & Kitchen Store and Wine Shop: Mon–Sat 9–6, Sun 11–4 CARDS MasterCard, Switch, Visa DISCOUNTS 5% for 5 cases or more DELIVERY

Free for complete cases or orders over £100 in most of mainland UK MINIMUM ORDER (mail order) 1 case EN PRIMEUR Bordeaux, Burgundy, Rhône. **G M T**
✪ **Star attractions** *Extensive list of personality-packed wines from around the world, chosen by a team of enthusiasts. Plenty from France, of course, but there's good stuff from Italy too, and Telmo Rodríguez, one of Spain's top winemakers, is well represented. New World wines include Ridge and Saintsbury from California, and Forrest Estate and Martinborough Vineyards from New Zealand.*

Aldi Stores

PO Box 26, Atherstone, Warwickshire CV9 2SH; 285 stores STORE LOCATION LINE 08705 134262 WEBSITE www.aldi-stores.co.uk HOURS Mon–Wed 9–6, Thurs–Fri 9–7, Sat 8.30–5.30, Sun 10–4 (selected stores) CARDS Switch, Visa (debit only)
✪ **Star attractions** *Aldi have some terrific bargains from around the world, with lots available under £3, but can also push the boat out for decent claret.*

Amey's Wines

83 Melford Road, Sudbury, Suffolk CO10 1JT (01787) 377144

HOURS Tue–Fri 9–5; Sat 9–4 CARDS AmEx, MasterCard, Switch, Visa DISCOUNTS 10% for a mixed dozen, 15% for 5 or more mixed cases DELIVERY Free within 10 miles of Sudbury for orders over £60. **G MT** ✪ **Star attractions** *Expect the unexpected in this well-chosen list of around 500 characterful wines: Gérard Depardieu's Condrieu (£20) rubs shoulders with Barbadillo's sherries, Montes Alpha Syrah from Chile (£12) and Penfolds Grange from Australia (£109).*

John Armit Wines

5 Royalty Studios, 105 Lancaster Road, London W11 1QF (020) 7908 0600 FAX (020) 7908 0601 E-MAIL info@armit.co.uk WEBSITE www.armit.co.uk HOURS Mon–Fri 9–6 CARDS MasterCard, Switch, Visa DELIVERY Free for orders over £180, otherwise £15 delivery charge MINIMUM ORDER 1 case EN PRIMEUR Bordeaux, Burgundy, Italy, Rhône. **C M T** ✪ **Star attractions** *Classy merchant with a star-studded list that's particularly strong on wines to go with food – from Italy, Burgundy and the Rhône, with some gems from Germany, Spain and the New World. For everyday drinking there's an own-label range from some top winemakers.*

ASDA

HEAD OFFICE Asda House, Southbank, Great Wilson Street, Leeds LS11 5AD (0113) 243 5435 FAX (0113) 241 8666 CUSTOMER SERVICE (0500) 100055; 279 stores WEBSITE www.asda.co.uk HOURS Selected stores open 24 hrs, see local store for details CARDS MasterCard, Switch, Visa DISCOUNTS Buy 6 bottles, save 10%; case deals: 10% off price including delivery DELIVERY Selected stores. ✪ **Star attractions** *Good-value basics – lots under a fiver – and the*

range now includes some interesting wines at £7+.

L'Assemblage

Pallant Court, 10 West Pallant, Chichester, West Sussex PO19 1TG (01243) 537775 FAX (01243) 538644 E-MAIL sales@lassemblage.co.uk WEBSITE www.lassemblage.co.uk HOURS Mon–Fri 9.30–6 CARDS MasterCard, Switch, Visa DELIVERY Free for orders over £500 MINIMUM ORDER 1 case EN PRIMEUR Bordeaux, Burgundy, Port, Rhône. **C M T** ✪ **Star attractions** *A fascinating list of fine wines, mostly from classic regions of France, especially Burgundy. Blue-chip wines at blue-chip prices.*

Australian Wine Club

MAIL ORDER PO Box 3079, Datchet, Slough SL3 9L2 0800 856 2004 FAX 0800 856 2114 E-MAIL orders@australianwine.co.uk WEBSITE www.australianwine.co.uk HOURS Mon–Fri 8am–9pm, Sat–Sun 9–6 CARDS AmEx, MasterCard, Switch, Visa, Diners DELIVERY £4.99 anywhere in UK mainland MINIMUM ORDER 1 mixed case. **M T** ✪ **Star attractions** *The original mail-order Aussie wine specialist, buzzing with top names.*

Averys Wine Merchants

4 High Street, Nailsea, Bristol BS48 1BT 08451 283797 FAX (01275) 811101 E-MAIL sales@averys.com WEBSITE www.averys.com • Shop and Cellars, 9 Culver Street, Bristol BS1 5LD (0117) 921 4146 E-MAIL cellars@averys.com HOURS Mon–Fri 9–7, Sat 9.30–5.30, Sun 10–4 CARDS AmEx, MasterCard, Switch, Visa DISCOUNTS Monthly mail order offers, Discover Wine with Averys 13th bottle free DELIVERY £5.95 per delivery address EN PRIMEUR Bordeaux, Burgundy, Port, Rhône. **C G M T** ✪ **Star attractions** *A small but very respectable selection from just*

about everywhere in France, Italy, Spain and Germany. Italy looks particularly promising and there's some good New World stuff, such as Felton Road from New Zealand and Hamilton Russell from South Africa.

Bacchus Wine

Warrington House Farm Barn, Warrington, Olney, Bucks MK46 4HN (01234) 711140 FAX (01234) 711199 E-MAIL wine@bacchus.co.uk WEBSITE www.bacchus.co.uk HOURS Mon–Fri 10.30–6.30, Sat 10.30–2 CARDS AmEx, Diners, MasterCard, Switch, Visa DELIVERY Free within 10 miles of Olney; elsewhere £10 1 case; £5 subsequent cases (maximum charge £20) MINIMUM ORDER 1 mixed case. G M T

✪ Star attractions *Plenty of unusual choices here: red wines from Austria, Beaujolais and Lebanon were on offer the last time I looked at the website, which is regularly updated. Splendid stuff from Italy, Spain, Burgundy – in fact from most of France – and you'll find many wines under £10.*

Ballantynes of Cowbridge

3 Westgate, Cowbridge, Vale of Glamorgan CF71 7AQ (01446) 774840 FAX (01446) 775253 E-MAIL richard@ballantynes.co.uk WEBSITE www.ballantynes.co.uk • 211–17 Cathedral Road, Cardiff, CF11 9PP (02920) 222202 HOURS Mon–Sat 9–5.30 CARDS MasterCard, Switch, Visa, Access DISCOUNTS 8% per case DELIVERY £9.99 for first case; £4.99 for subsequent cases EN PRIMEUR Bordeaux, Burgundy, Italy, Rhône. C G M T

✪ Star attractions *Italy, Burgundy and Languedoc-Roussillon are stunning, most regions of France are well represented, and there's some terrific stuff from Australia, New Zealand, Spain, California and South Africa.*

Balls Brothers

313 Cambridge Heath Road, London E2 9LQ (020) 7739 6466 FAX 0870 243 9775 DIRECT SALES (020) 7739 1642 E-MAIL wine@ballsbrothers.co.uk WEBSITE www.ballsbrothers.co.uk HOURS Mon–Fri 9–5.30 CARDS AmEx, Diners, MasterCard, Switch, Visa DELIVERY Free 1 case or more locally; £8 1 case, free 2 cases or more, England, Wales and Scottish Lowlands; islands and Scottish Highlands phone for details. G M T

✪ Star attractions *French specialist – you'll find something of interest from most regions – with older vintages available. Spain and Australia are also very good. Many of the wines can be enjoyed in Balls Brothers' London wine bars.*

H & H Bancroft Wines

1 China Wharf, 29 Mill Street, London SE1 2BQ (020) 7232 5450 FAX (020) 7232 5451 E-MAIL sales@handhbancroftwines.com WEBSITE www.bancroftwines.com HOURS Mon–Fri 9–5.30 CARDS Delta, MasterCard, Switch, Visa DISCOUNTS Negotiable DELIVERY £11.75 for 1–2 cases in mainland UK; free 3 cases or more MINIMUM ORDER 1 case EN PRIMEUR Bordeaux, Burgundy, Rhône. C M T

✪ Star attractions *Bancroft are UK agents for an impressive flotilla of French winemakers: Burgundy, Rhône, Loire and some interesting wines from southern France. Italy looks promising, too. A separate fine wine list includes Bordeaux back to 1945, plus top names from Burgundy and the Rhône.*

Bat & Bottle

MAIL ORDER 24d Pillings Road, Oakham, Rutland LE15 6QF 0845 108 4407 /01572 759735 FAX 0870 458 2505 E-MAIL post@batwine.co.uk WEBSITE www.batwine.co.uk HOURS Mon–Thurs 9–5, Fri 9–7, Sat 10–5,

CARDS MasterCard, Switch, Visa. **G M T**
✪ **Star attractions** *Ben and Emma Robson specialize in Italy, and in characterful wines from small producers discovered on their regular visits to the country. An inspired and inspiring list.*

Bennetts Fine Wines

High Street, Chipping Campden, Glos GL55 6AG (01386) 840392 FAX (01386) 840974 E-MAIL enquiries@bennettsfinewines.com WEBSITE www.bennettsfinewines.com HOURS Tues–Fri 10–6, Sat 9.30–6 CARDS MasterCard, Switch, Visa, Access DISCOUNTS On collected orders of 1 case or more DELIVERY £6 per case, minimum charge £12 EN PRIMEUR Burgundy, California, Rhône, New Zealand. **G M T**
✪ **Star attractions** *Given the calibre of the producers, the prices are very fair: there's certainly lots to choose from at around £10. France and Italy have the lion's share, but Germany, Spain and Portugal look good too. New World wines are similarly high up the quality scale, with the likes of Kumeu River and Isabel Estate from New Zealand, Plantagenet and Cullen from Australia, Seghesio from California and Domaine Drouhin from Oregon.*

Berkmann Wine Cellars

10–12 Brewery Road, London N7 9NH (020) 7609 4711 FAX (020) 7607 0018 • Brunel Park, Vincients Road, Bumpers Farm, Chippenham, Wiltshire SN14 6NQ (01249) 463501 • Brian Coad Wine Cellars, 41b Valley Road, Plympton, Plymouth, Devon PL7 1RF (01752) 334970 FAX (01752) 346540 • Pagendam Pratt Wine Cellars, 16 Marston Moor Business Park, Rudgate, Tockwith, N. Yorks YO26 7QF (01423) 337567 FAX (01423) 357568 • T M Robertson Wine Cellars, Unit 12, A1 Industrial Estate, 232 Sir Harry Lauder Road, Portobello, Edinburgh EH15 2QA

(0131) 657 6390 FAX (0131) 657 6389 FAX (01249) 463502 E-MAIL info@berkmann.co.uk WEBSITE www.berkmann.co.uk HOURS Mon–Fri 9–5.30 CARDS MasterCard, Switch, Visa DISCOUNTS £3 per unmixed case collected DELIVERY Free for orders over £100 to UK mainland (excluding the Highlands) MINIMUM ORDER 1 mixed case. **C G M**
✪ **Star attractions** *Wow! Where do you start on a list that includes Mexico, Corsica and India? Italy, perhaps, since Berkmann is the UK agent for, among others, Antinori, Maculan, Mastroberardino, Masi and Tasca d'Almerita, so there are some fab Italian wines here. Spain has Marqués de Griñon, Portugal has Casa Ferreirinha. New World wines include some top stuff from Australia, New Zealand, South Africa and California. But France hasn't been forgotten: affordable claret and Burgundy, Alsace, Beaujolais, Loire … need I go on?*

Berry Bros. & Rudd

3 St James's Street, London SW1A 1EG (020) 7396 9600 FAX (020) 7396 9611 ORDERS OFFICE 0870 900 4300 (lines open Mon–Fri 9–6, ORDERS FAX 0870 900 4301 • Berrys' Wine Shop, (Sat 10-4) Hamilton Close, Houndmills, Basingstoke, Hants RG21 6YB (01256) 323566 • Terminal 3 departures, Heathrow Airport, TW6 1JH (020) 8564 8361 • Terminal 4 departures, Heathrow, TW6 3XA (020) 8754 1961 E-MAIL orders@bbr.com WEBSITE www.bbr.com HOURS St James's Street: Mon–Fri 10–6, Sat 10–4; Berrys' Wine Shop: Mon–Thur 10–6, Fri 10–7, Sat 10–4; Heathrow: daily 6am–10pm CARDS AmEx, Diners, MasterCard, Switch, Visa DISCOUNTS Variable DELIVERY Free for orders of £180 or more, otherwise £10 EN PRIMEUR Bordeaux, Burgundy, Rhône. **C G M T**

✪ Star attractions *The shop in St James's is the very image of a traditional wine merchant, but Berry Bros. also has one of the best websites around. The Blue List covers old, rare fine wines while the main list is both classy and wide-ranging: there's an emphasis on the classic regions of France; smaller but equally tempting selections from just about everywhere else. Not everything is expensive: Berrys' Own Selection is extensive, with a Good Ordinary Claret at £5.25.*

Bibendum Wine

113 Regents Park Road, London NW1 8UR (020) 7449 4120 **FAX** (020) 7449 4121 **E-MAIL** sales@bibendum-wine.co.uk **WEBSITE** www.bibendum-wine.co.uk **HOURS** Mon–Fri 9–6 **CARDS** MasterCard, Switch, Visa **DELIVERY** Free throughout mainland UK for orders over £250, otherwise £15 **EN PRIMEUR** Bordeaux, Burgundy, New World, Rhône, Port. **M T**

✪ Star attractions *Bibendum looks for wines that nobody else is shipping – although that's not to say you won't find them elsewhere, since Bibendum supply the trade as well as private customers. Equally strong in the Old World and the New: Huet in Vouvray, Lageder in Alto Adige and Brundlmayer in Austria are matched by d'Arenberg and Katnook from Australia and Catena Zapata from Argentina.*

Booths Supermarkets

4 Fishergate, Preston PR1 3LJ (01772) 251701 **FAX** (01772) 204316; 26 stores across the North of England **E-MAIL** admin@booths-supermarkets.co.uk **WEBSITE** www.booths-supermarkets.co.uk and www.booths-wine.co.uk **HOURS** Office: Mon–Fri 8.30–5; shop hours vary **CARDS** AmEx, Electron, MasterCard, Switch, Solo, Visa **DISCOUNTS** 5% off any 6 bottles. **G T**

✪ Star attractions *A list for any merchant to be proud of, never mind a supermarket. There's plenty under £4, but if you're occasionally prepared to hand over £7–9 you'll find some really interesting stuff.*

Bordeaux Index

MAIL ORDER 6th Floor, 159–173 St John Street, London EC1V 4QJ (020) 7253 2110 **FAX** (020) 7490 1995 **E-MAIL** sales@bordeauxindex.com **WEBSITE** www.bordeauxindex.com **HOURS** Mon–Fri 8.30–6 **CARDS** AmEx, MasterCard, Switch, Visa, JCB (transaction fees apply) **DELIVERY** (Private sales only) free for orders over £2,000 UK mainland; others at cost **MINIMUM ORDER** £500 **EN PRIMEUR** Bordeaux, Burgundy, Rhône, Italy. **C T**

✪ Star attractions *A serious list for serious spenders. Pages and pages of red Bordeaux and, in spite of the company name, stacks of top Burgundies and Rhônes. Italy and Australia are looking increasingly interesting.*

Budgens Stores

HEAD OFFICE Stonefield Way, Ruislip, Middlesex HA4 0JR (020) 8422 9511 **FAX** (020) 8864 2800, for nearest store call 0800 526002; 234 stores mainly in Southern England and East Anglia **E-MAIL** info@ budgens.co.uk **WEBSITE** www.budgens.co.uk **HOURS** Vary according to location (55 stores open 24 hours); usually Mon–Sat 8–8, Sun 10–4 **CARDS** MasterCard, Solo, Switch, Visa. **G**

✪ Star attractions *You can feel reasonably confident of going into a store and coming out with some wine you'd actually like to drink, at bargain-basement prices upwards.*

The Butlers Wine Cellar

247 Queens Park Road, Brighton BN2 9XJ (01273) 698724 **FAX** (01273) 622761 **E-MAIL** henry@butlers-winecellar.co.uk **WEBSITE** www.butlers-winecellar.co.uk

Young Wine Writer Award 2006

The Circle of Wine Writers is pleased to offer this annual award of £1000, sponsored by Websters International Publishers and the Australian Wine Bureau, to help develop promising young UK-based wine writers. The award is to enable a writer to travel to a wine region of his or her choice to gain first-hand experience and to develop a book or article based on that experience. It is open to any wine writer under 30 who has not yet had a book published and is not yet an established columnist or regular contributor to a magazine. He or she should be able to demonstrate wine-writing ability and commitment to popular consumer wine writing.

Details of how to enter can be found at
www.websters.co.uk
or, for further information, please contact
Fiona Holman at Websters International Publishers
Second Floor, Axe and Bottle Court, 70 Newcomen Street
London SE1 1YT. Tel: 020 7940 4720
or email fionaho@websters.co.uk

Information about the award and previous winners can be found at
www.websters.co.uk

HOURS Tue–Wed 10–6, Thur–Sat 10–7 **CARDS** AmEx, MasterCard, Switch, Visa **DELIVERY** Free locally 1 case or more; free UK mainland 3 cases or more **EN PRIMEUR** Bordeaux. **G M T ✪ Star attractions** *The regular list is full of fascinating stuff, all personally chosen by Henry Butler; Italy and Spain look strong, and there's Breaky Bottom from England. But it's the bin end list that's the main point, guaranteed to delight Bordeaux enthusiasts. Prices are affordable – you can get some great surprises here for only £20 – and although the risk is there, you could get a very good bottle: you'll only find out by* buying it. *You want a 35-year-old wine for only £25? Here's where to come. And – in smaller numbers – there's excellent Burgundy, Rhône, Loire and Germany. You'll need to look at the website or join the mailing list, as these odds and ends change all the time.*

Anthony Byrne
MAIL ORDER Ramsey Business Park, Stocking Fen Road, Ramsey, Cambs PE26 2UR (01487) 814555 **FAX** (01487) 814962 **E-MAIL** anthony@abfw.co.uk or claude@abfw.co.uk **WEBSITE** www.abfw.co.uk **HOURS** Mon–Fri 9–5.30 **CARDS** None

DISCOUNTS available on cases DELIVERY Free 5 cases or more, or orders of £250 or more; otherwise £12 MINIMUM ORDER 1 case EN PRIMEUR Bordeaux, Burgundy, Rhône. C M T

✪ Star attractions *A serious list of Burgundy; Loire from top growers such as Serge Dagueneau; and from Alsace there are enough Zind-Humbrecht wines to sink a ship. Interesting French wines also come from Provence (Ch. de Pibarnon) and the Rhône (Alain Graillot). Increasing coverage of South Africa.*

D Byrne & Co

Victoria Buildings, 12 King Street, Clitheroe, Lancs BB7 2EP (01200) 423152 HOURS Mon–Sat 8.30–6 CARDS MasterCard, Switch, Visa DELIVERY Free within 50 miles; nationally £10 1st case, £5 subsequent cases EN PRIMEUR Bordeaux, Burgundy, Rhône, Germany. G M T

✪ Star attractions *One of northern England's best wine merchants, with a hugely impressive range. Clarets back to 1982, stacks of Burgundy, faultless Loire and Rhône, Germany, Spain, USA (not just California) and many, many more. I urge you to go and see for yourself.*

Cape Wine and Food

77 Laleham Road, Staines, Middx TW18 2EA (01784) 451860 FAX (01784) 469267 E-MAIL ross@capewineandfood.com WEBSITE www.capewineandfood.com HOURS Mon–Sat 10–6 CARDS AmEx, MasterCard, Switch, Visa DISCOUNTS buy 12 bottles, pay for 11 DELIVERY £7.55 per case. G M T

✪ Star attractions *South African wines from 80 estates, including top names such as Graham Beck, Iona, Thelema and Vergelegen.*

Cave Cru Classé

MAIL ORDER Unit 3b Trowbray House, Weston Street, London SE1 3QB

(020) 7378 8579 FAX (020) 7378 8544 E-MAIL enquiries@ccc.co.uk WEBSITE www.cave-cru-classe.com HOURS Mon–Fri 9–5.30 CARDS AmEx, MasterCard, Visa DELIVERY £10 per order in London; at cost elsewhere MINIMUM ORDER 1 mixed case EN PRIMEUR Bordeaux. M T

✪ Star attractions *An excellent, constantly changing selection of clarets. If Burgundy or Rhône are your wines of choice, there are pages of top names to choose from. Italy and port look starry, too.*

Les Caves de Pyrene

Pew Corner, Old Portsmouth Road, Artington, Guildford GU3 1LP (office) (01483) 538820 (shop) (01483) 554750 FAX (01483) 455068 E-MAIL sales@lescaves.co.uk WEBSITE www.lescaves.co.uk HOURS (office) Mon–Sat 9–5 (shop) Mon–Sat 9–7 CARDS MasterCard, Switch, Visa DELIVERY Free for orders over £200 within M25, elsewhere at cost DISCOUNTS negotiable MINIMUM ORDER 1 mixed case EN PRIMEUR South-West France. G M T

✪ Star attractions *Excellent operation, devoted to seeking out top wines from all over southern France. Other areas of France, especially the Loire, are equally good. And there's Armagnac dating back to 1893!*

ChateauOnline

MAIL ORDER BP68, 39602 Arbois Cedex, France (0033) 3 84 66 42 21 FAX (0033) 1 55 30 31 41 CUSTOMER SERVICE 0800 169 2736 WEBSITE www.chateauonline.com HOURS Mon–Fri 8–11.30, 12.30–4.30 CARDS AmEx, MasterCard, Switch, Visa DELIVERY £7.99 per consignment EN PRIMEUR Bordeaux, Burgundy, Languedoc-Roussillon.

✪ Star attractions *French specialist, with an impressive list of over 3,000 wines. Easy-to-use website with a well-thought-out range of mixed cases, frequent special offers and bin end sales.*

Cockburns of Leith (incorporating J E Hogg)

Cockburn House, Unit 3, Abbeyhill Industrial Estate, Abbeyhill, Edinburgh EH8 8HL (0131) 661 8400 FAX (0131) 661 6333 • 382 Morningside Road, Edinburgh EH10 5HX (0131) 446 0700 E-MAIL sales@winelist.co.uk
WEBSITE www.winelist.co.uk
HOURS Mon–Fri 9–6; Sat 10–5
CARDS MasterCard, Switch, Visa
DELIVERY Free 12 or more bottles within Edinburgh; elsewhere £7 1–2 cases, free 3 cases or more EN PRIMEUR Bordeaux, Burgundy. **G T**
✪ Star attractions *Clarets at bargain prices – in fact wines from all over France, including plenty of vins de pays. Among other countries New Zealand looks promising, and there's a great range of sherries.*

Connolly's Wine Merchants

Arch 13, 220 Livery Street, Birmingham B3 1EU (0121) 236 9269/3837 FAX (0121) 233 2339 E-MAIL sales@connollyswine.co.uk
WEBSITE www.connollyswine.co.uk
HOURS Mon–Fri 9–5.30, Sat 10–4
CARDS AmEx, MasterCard, Switch, Visa DELIVERY Surcharge outside Birmingham area DISCOUNTS 10% for cash & carry EN PRIMEUR Burgundy. **G M T**
✪ Star attractions *There's something for everyone here. Burgundy, Bordeaux and the Rhône all look very good; and there are top names from Germany (Dr Loosen, Selbach-Oster), Italy (Isole e Olena, Allegrini), Spain (Artadi, Marqués de Riscal) and California (Bonny Doon, Saintsbury, Ridge). Monthly tutored tastings and winemaker dinners.*

The Co-operative Group

HEAD OFFICE New Century House, Manchester M60 4ES Freephone 0800 068 6727 for stock details FAX (0161) 827 5117; approx. 3,000 licensed stores E-MAIL customer relations@co-op.co.uk WEBSITE www.co-op.co.uk HOURS Variable CARDS Variable • ONLINE WINE STORE www.co-opdrinks2u.com TELEPHONE 0845 090 2222 CARDS AmEx, MasterCard, Solo, Switch, Visa DELIVERY Within 7 days mainland UK £4.99 (UK islands and N. Ireland £23); Saturday delivery (major towns only) £26
✪ Star attractions *Champions of organic and Fairtrade wines. Chile, Australia, South Africa and California all deliver tasty wine for around £5.*

Corney & Barrow

HEAD OFFICE No. 1 Thomas More Street, London E1W 1YZ (020) 7265 2400 FAX (020) 7265 2539
• 194 Kensington Park Road, London W11 2ES (020) 7221 5122
• Corney & Barrow East Anglia, Belvoir House, High Street, Newmarket CB8 8DH (01638) 600000 • Corney & Barrow (Scotland) with Whighams of Ayr, 8 Academy Street, Ayr KA7 1HT (01292) 267000, and Oxenfoord Castle, by Pathhead, Mid Lothian, EH37 5UD (01875) 321921
E-MAIL wine@corbar.co.uk
WEBSITE www.corneyand barrow.com HOURS Mon–Fri 8–6 (24-hr answering machine); Kensington Mon–Fri 10.30–9, Sat 9.30–8; Newmarket Mon–Sat 9–6; Edinburgh Mon–Fri 9–6; Ayr Mon–Fri 9–6, Sat 9.30–5.30 CARDS AmEx, MasterCard, Maestro, Visa DELIVERY Free 24 or more bottles within M25 boundary, elsewhere free 36 or more bottles or for orders above £200. Otherwise £9 + VAT per delivery. For Scotland and East Anglia, please contact the relevant office
EN PRIMEUR Bordeaux, Burgundy, Champagne, Rhône, Italy, Spain.
C G M T

✪ **Star attractions** *If you want certain Pomerols like Pétrus, Trotanoy, la Fleur-Pétrus and Latour à Pomerol, Corney & Barrow, by Royal Appointment, is where you have to come. At least, if you want them en primeur. Burgundy kicks off with Domaine de la Romanée-Conti and proceeds via names like Domaine Trapet and Domaine Leflaive. The rest of Europe is equally impressive; with Australia, South Africa and South America hot on their heels. Wines in every price bracket; try them out at Corney & Barrow wine bars in London.*

Croque-en-Bouche

Col House, Walwyn Road, Upper Colwall, Malvern, Worcestershire WR13 6PR (01684) 540011 **FAX** (08707) 066282 **E-MAIL** mail@croque-en-bouche.co.uk **WEBSITE** www.croque-en-bouche. co.uk **HOURS** By appointment 7 days a week **CARDS** MasterCard, Switch, Visa **DISCOUNTS** 3% for orders over £500 if paid in cash or by Switch or Delta **DELIVERY** Free locally; elsewhere £5 per consignment; free in England and Wales for orders over £500 if paid by credit card **MINIMUM ORDER** 1 mixed case. **M**
✪ **Star attractions** *A wonderful list, including older wines. Mature Australian reds from the 1990s; terrific stuff from the Rhône – Château Beaucastel's Châteauneuf-du-Pape going back to 1979; some top clarets; and a generous sprinkling from other parts of the world. Sweet wines include marvellously mature Sauternes and Loire wines.*

Devigne Wines

Mas Y Coed, 13 Llanerchydol Park, Welshpool SY21 9QE (01938) 553478 **FAX** (01938) 556831 **E-MAIL** info@devignewines.co.uk **WEBSITE** www.devignewines.co.uk **HOURS** Mon–Fri 10–6 (telephone 7 days) **CARDS** MasterCard, Switch,

Visa **DISCOUNTS** selected mixed cases at introductory rate **DELIVERY** free for orders over £300, otherwise £6.50 per consignment **M**
✪ **Star attractions** *Small list specializing in French wines: 12 different rosés and 17 traditional-(Champagne) method sparkling wines from all over France as well as red Gaillac from the South-West and a range of Languedoc reds.*

Direct Wine Shipments

5–7 Corporation Square, Belfast, N Ireland BT1 3AJ (028) 9050 8000 **FAX** (028) 9050 8004 **E-MAIL** shop@directwine.co.uk **WEBSITE** www.directwine.co.uk **HOURS** Mon–Fri 9–6.30 (Thur 10–8), Sat 9.30–5.30 **CARDS** MasterCard, Switch, Visa **DISCOUNTS** 10% in the form of complimentary wine with each case **DELIVERY** Free N Ireland 1 case or more, variable delivery charge for UK mainland depending on customer spend **EN PRIMEUR** Bordeaux, Burgundy, Rhône. **C M T**
✪ **Star attractions** *Rhône, Spain, Australia and Burgundy look outstanding, Italy and Germany are not far behind, and from Chile there's Santa Rita and Miguel Torres. In fact there's good stuff from pretty well everywhere. Wine courses, tastings and expert advice.*

Dodici

PO Box 428, Harpenden, Hertfordshire AL5 3ZT (01582) 713004 **FAX** (01582) 767991 **E-MAIL** angus@dodici.co.uk **WEBSITE** www.dodici.co.uk **HOURS** Mon–Fri 9–6.30 (Thur 10–8), Sat 9.30–5.30 **CARDS** MasterCard, Switch, Visa **DELIVERY** Free locally. **M T**
✪ **Star attractions** *There's such a wealth of interesting wine in Italy that it's really encouraging to find an independent company seeking out jewels that are usually hidden to the British consumer. Choose a pre-mixed case or create your own*

*from a terrific list that includes
plenty of wines at £6–7.*

Domaine Direct

8 Cynthia Street, London N1 9JF
(020) 7837 1142 FAX (020) 7837
8605 E-MAIL mail@domainedirect.
co.uk WEBSITE www.domainedirect.
co.uk HOURS 8.30–6 or answering
machine CARDS MasterCard,
Switch, Visa DELIVERY Free London;
elsewhere in UK mainland 1 case
£11.50, 2 cases £15, or more free
MINIMUM ORDER 1 mixed case
EN PRIMEUR Burgundy. M T
✪ Star attractions *Sensational
Burgundy list. From Australia you'll
find wines from the Leeuwin Estate;
from California there's
Spottswoode, Etude and Nalle.*

Farr Vintners

220 Queenstown Road, Battersea,
London, SW8 4LP (020) 7821 2000
FAX (020) 7821 2020 E-MAIL
sales@farrvintners.com
WEBSITE www.farrvintners.com
HOURS Mon–Fri 10–6 CARDS Switch
DELIVERY London £1 per case (min
£14); elsewhere at cost MINIMUM
ORDER £500 + VAT
EN PRIMEUR Bordeaux. C M
✪ Star attractions *A fantastic list
of the world's finest wines. The
majority is Bordeaux, but you'll
also find top stuff and older
vintages of white Burgundy and
red Rhône, Italy (Gaja, Sassicaia),
Australia and California (Araujo,
Dominus).*

Irma Fingal-Rock

64 Monnow Street, Monmouth
NP25 3EN TEL & FAX 01600 712372
E-MAIL tom@pinotnoir.co.uk
WEBSITE www.pinotnoir.co.uk
HOURS Mon 9.30–1.30, Thurs & Fri
9.30–5.30, Sat 9.30–5 CARDS
MasterCard, Switch, Visa DISCOUNTS
5% for at least 12 bottles collected
from shop, 7.5% for collected orders
over £500, 10% for collected orders
over £1,200 DELIVERY Free locally

(within 30 miles); orders further
afield free if over £100. G M T
✪ Star attractions *A merchant who
knows the highways and byways of
French wine better than most. The
list's great strength is Burgundy,
from some very good growers and
priced between £6 and £34. Small
but tempting selections from other
French regions, as well as Italy,
Spain, Portugal and the New World.
Two local (yes, Welsh) producers are
also represented.*

Flagship Wines

417 Hatfield Road, St Albans,
Hertfordshire AL4 0XP (01727)
865309 E-MAIL
info@flagshipwines.co.uk WEBSITE
www.flagshipwines.co.uk HOURS
10–6 Mon–Sat CARDS MasterCard,
Switch, Visa DELIVERY Free within 5
miles of St Albans; £8.50 per case
elsewhere in UK mainland.
G M T
✪ Star attractions *Well-run
independent whose prices can
match those of the supermarkets –
and you get the friendly, well-
informed advice of boss Julia
Jenkins thrown in for free. Good
Chilean and French basics,
interesting Italians, and strongest in
Spain, Australia and Portugal.*

Le Fleming Wines

MAIL ORDER 19 Spenser Road,
Harpenden, Hertfordshire AL5 5NW
(01582) 760125 E-MAIL cherry@
leflemingwines.co.uk WEBSITE
www.leflemingwines.co.uk
HOURS 24-hour answering machine
DISCOUNTS 5% on large orders
DELIVERY Free locally MINIMUM
ORDER 1 case. G
✪ Star attractions *Australia looks
terrific here, with lots of serious and
not so serious wines. South Africa,
too, is good, with wines from
Hamilton Russell and Thelema. The
list is basically the New World and
France, plus short but focused
selections from Italy and Spain.*

The Flying Corkscrew

Leighton Buzzard Road, Water End,
Nr Hemel Hempstead,
Hertfordshire HP1 3BD
(01442) 412311 **FAX** (01442) 412313
E-MAIL sales@flyingcorkscrew.com
WEBSITE www.flyingcorkscrew.com
HOURS Mon–Wed 10–7, Thurs–Fri
10–8, Sat 10–7, Sun 11–5 **CARDS**
AmEx, MasterCard, Switch, Visa
DISCOUNTS 10% on case **DELIVERY**
Free locally, £15 per case UK
mainland. **G M T**
✪ **Star attractions** *A very stylish
shop with friendly, knowledgeable
staff and an extensive and*

THE FLYING CORKSCREW
THE VERY INDEPENDENT WINE MERCHANT

Independent
WINE MERCHANT OF THE
YEAR 2003

Central England
WINE MERCHANT OF THE
YEAR 2003

Runner up – Eastern England
WINE MERCHANT OF THE
YEAR 2004

We have loads of parking.
Comfy area with wine reference library and
toys to amuse the kids!

Our knowledgeable staff can give you
advice about wines from all over the world.
Buy by the bottle or by the case.
10% case discount
(12 bottles – may be mixed)

Imported bottled beers
Gift ideas, chocolates, condiments etc.
Mail order - national delivery available.

**Leighton Buzzard Road, Water End
Nr. Hemel Hempstead HP1 3BD
Tel: 01442 412311
info@flyingcorkscrew.com
www.flyingcorkscrew.com**

*imaginative range of wines. If
you're local, look out for tastings led
by experts and winemakers such as
Randall Grahm of Bonny Doon, and
Douro specialist Dirk Niepoort.*

Fortnum & Mason

181 Piccadilly, London W1A 1ER (020)
7734 8040 **FAX** (020) 7437 3278
ORDERING LINE 0845 300 1707
E-MAIL info@fortnumandmason.
co.uk **WEBSITE** www.fortnumand
mason.co.uk **HOURS** Mon–Sat
10–6.30, Sun 12–6 (Food Hall and
Patio Restaurant only) **CARDS**
AmEx, Diners, MasterCard, Switch,
Visa **DISCOUNTS** 1 free bottle per
unmixed dozen **DELIVERY** £7 per
delivery address **EN PRIMEUR**
Bordeaux. **M T**
✪ **Star attractions** *Champagne,
Bordeaux and Burgundy are the
leaders of a very smart pack, but
there are names to impress from just
about everywhere, including the
cream of the crop from Italy,
Germany, Australia, New Zealand,
South Africa and California.
Impeccably sourced own-label range.*

Friarwood

26 New King's Road, London SW6
4ST (020) 7736 2628 **FAX** (020)
7731 0411 • 16 Dock St, Leith,
Edinburgh, EH6 6EY (0131) 554 4159
FAX (0131) 554 6703 **E-MAIL**
sales@friarwood.com;
edinbugh@friarwood.com
WEBSITE www.friarwood.com
HOURS Mon–Sat 10–7 **CARDS** AmEx,
Diners, MasterCard, Switch, Visa,
Solo, Electron **DISCOUNTS** 5% on
mixed cases, 10% unmixed
DELIVERY (London) Free within
M25 and on orders over £250 in
mainland UK (Edinburgh) free
locally and for 2 cases or more
elsewhere (under 2 cases at cost)
EN PRIMEUR Bordeaux. **C G M T**
✪ **Star attractions** *The focus is
Bordeaux, including a good
selection of petits châteaux as well
as classed growths; vintages*

*available go back to 1982, or 1967
for Yquem. Burgundy and other
French regions are strong too, but
this year I've been particularly
impressed by the wines they've
chosen from independent producers
in Chile (Haras de Pirque), New
Zealand (Clifford Bay) and Australia
(Belgravia). Armagnacs back to 1940
round off this imaginative list.*

Gauntleys

4 High Street, Exchange Arcade,
Nottingham NG1 2ET (0115) 911
0555 FAX (0115) 911 0557
E-MAIL rhone@gauntleywine.com
WEBSITE www.gauntleywine.com
HOURS Mon–Sat 9–5.30 CARDS
MasterCard, Switch, Visa DELIVERY
Free within Nottingham area,
otherwise 1–3 cases £9.50, 4 or
more cases free MINIMUM ORDER 1
case EN PRIMEUR Alsace, Burgundy,
Italy, Loire, Rhône, southern France,
Spain. M T

✿ Star attractions *They've won
awards for their Rhône list, but it
doesn't stop there: Alsace, Loire,
Burgundy, southern France, Spain
and Italy are all top-notch. No
Bordeaux. Champagne is Vilmart's
wonderfully big, rich wines.*

Goedhuis & Co

6 Rudolf Place, Miles Street,
London SW8 1RP (020) 7793
7900 FAX (020) 7793 7170
E-MAIL sales@goedhuis.com
WEBSITE www.goedhuis.com
HOURS Mon–Fri 9–5.30 CARDS
AmEx, MasterCard, Switch, Visa
DELIVERY Free 3 cases or more,
otherwise £10 England, elsewhere
at cost MINIMUM ORDER 1 unmixed
case EN PRIMEUR Bordeaux,
Burgundy. C G M T

✿ Star attractions *Fine wine
specialist. Bordeaux, Burgundy and
the Rhône are the core of the list,
but everything is good, and if you
buy your everyday wines here you'll
get very good quality, plus friendly,
expert advice.*

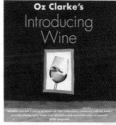
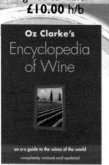

Great Northern Wine

The Warehouse, Blossomgate, Ripon, N. Yorks HG4 2AJ (01765) 606767 FAX (01765) 609151 E-MAIL info@greatnorthern wine.com HOURS Mon–Fri 9–6, Sat 9–5.30 CARDS AmEx, MasterCard, Switch, Visa DISCOUNTS 10% on case quantities DELIVERY Free locally, elsewhere at cost. **G M T**
✪ Star attractions *A sound list that mixes well-known and less familiar names, specializing in Old World wines: Portugal, Spain, France and Italy look highly desirable, but are well supported by Australia, New Zealand and South Africa.*

Great Western Wine

The Wine Warehouse, Wells Road, Bath BA2 3AP (01225) 322810 FAX (01225) 442139 E-MAIL retail@greatwesternwine.co.uk WEBSITE www.greatwesternwine. co.uk HOURS Mon–Fri 10–7, Sat 10–6 CARDS AmEx, MasterCard, Switch, Visa DISCOUNTS Negotiable DELIVERY Free 3 or more cases, otherwise £6 MINIMUM ORDER 1 mixed case EN PRIMEUR Australia, Bordeaux, Burgundy, Rioja. **C G M T**
✪ Star attractions *Great Western brings in wines from individual growers around the world. Highlights include Bonnefond and Gilles Robin from the Rhône, Glaetzer and Heartland from Australia, Carrick from New Zealand – and this year they've ventured as far as Uruguay. Frequent events and tastings.*

Peter Green & Co

37A/B Warrender Park Road, Edinburgh EH9 1HJ (0131) 229 5925 FAX (0131) 229 0606 E-MAIL shop@petergreenwines.com HOURS Tues–Thur 10–6.30, Fri 10–7.30, Sat 10–6.30 CARDS MasterCard, Switch, Visa DISCOUNTS 5% on unmixed half-dozens DELIVERY Free in Edinburgh MINIMUM ORDER (For delivery) 1 case. **G T**
✪ Star attractions *Extensive, well-chosen and adventurous list from all over the world.*

Halifax Wine Company

18 Prescott Street, Halifax, West Yorkshire HX1 2LG (01422) 256333 E-MAIL andy@halifaxwinecompany.com WEBSITE www.halifaxwinecompany.com HOURS Tues–Fri 9.30–6, Sat 9–5 CARDS Switch, Access, MasterCard, Visa DISCOUNTS 8% on 12 bottles or more for personal callers to the shop DELIVERY Free locally on orders over £75; rest of UK mainland, £9.95 for 6 bottles or less; £7.95 first case. **G M T**
✪ Star attractions *Exciting and extremely wide-ranging list: I don't know of many places you'd find 70 wines from Portugal and a similar number from Spain; there are even 10 wines from Greece. Champagnes*

Blaise Carron
*Just one of the producers we have
discovered in France, South Africa
and Australia capable of making
wine as individual as themselves*

Roger Harris Wines,
delivering high quality wines
directly to your door since 1974

PLEASE PHONE TO PLACE AN ORDER OR IF YOU WISH TO
DISCUSS YOUR WINE REQUIREMENTS

**ROGER
HARRIS**
Wines

Telephone: 01603 880171
Fax: 01603 880291
E-mail: sales@rogerharriswines.co.uk
www.rogerharriswines.co.uk
Loke Farm, Weston Longville, Norwich NR9 5LG

---

*include Billecart-Salmon, and other
regions of France are just as
carefully chosen.*

Roger Harris Wines

Loke Farm, Weston Longville,
Norfolk NR9 5LG (01603) 880171
FAX (01603) 880291 E-MAIL
sales@rogerharriswines.co.uk
WEBSITE www.rogerharris
wines.co.uk HOURS Mon–Fri 9–5
CARDS AmEx, MasterCard, Visa
DELIVERY next working day UK
mainland, £3 for orders up to £110,
£2 up to £160, free over £160
MINIMUM ORDER 1 mixed case. M
✪ Star attractions *Beaujolais-loving
family business – Britain's
acknowledged experts in this area.
The list also ventures into the
Mâconnais, Champagne and the
south of France. Now includes small
producers from Australia, New
Zealand and South Africa.*

Harvey Nichols

109–125 Knightsbridge, London
SW1X 7RJ (020) 7235 5000 • The
Mailbox, 31–32 Wharfside Street,
Birmingham B1 1RE (0121) 616 6000

• 30–34 St Andrew Square,
Edinburgh EH2 3AD (0131) 524 8388
• 107–111 Briggate, Leeds LS1 6AZ
(0113) 204 8888 • 21 New Cathedral
Street, Manchester M3 1RE (0161)
828 8888 E-MAIL wineshop@
harveynichols.com WEBSITE
www.harveynichols.com
HOURS (London) Mon–Fri 10–8,
Sat 10–7, Sun 12–6 (Birmingham)
Mon-Wed 10–6, Thurs 10–8,
Fri–Sat 10–7, Sun 11–5 (Edinburgh)
Mon–Wed 10–6, Thurs 10–8,
Fri, Sat 10–7, Sun 11–5 (Leeds)
Mon–Wed 10–6, Thurs–Fri 10–7,
Sat 9–7, Sun 12–6 (Manchester)
Mon, Wed, Fri 10–7, Thurs 10–8,
Sat 9–7, Sun 12–6 CARDS AmEx,
MasterCard, Switch, Visa.
✪ Star attractions *Top names
from France, Italy and California,
especially for sought-after producers
such as Harlan, Kistler and Turley.*

Haynes Hanson & Clark

Sheep Street, Stow-on-the-Wold,
Glos GL54 1AA (01451) 870808
FAX (01451) 870508 • 25 Eccleston
Street, London SW1W 9NP (020)
7259 0102 FAX (020) 7259 0103

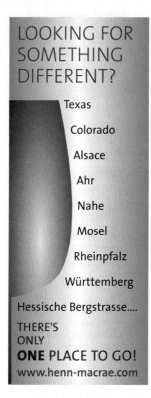

LOOKING FOR
SOMETHING
DIFFERENT?

Texas

Colorado

Alsace

Ahr

Nahe

Mosel

Rheinpfalz

Württemberg

Hessische Bergstrasse....

THERE'S
ONLY
ONE PLACE TO GO!
www.henn-macrae.com

E-MAIL stow@hhandc.co.uk or london@hhandc.co.uk **WEBSITE** www.hhandc.co.uk **HOURS** (Stow) Mon–Fri 9–6, Sat 9–5.30 (London) Mon–Fri 9–7 **CARDS** AmEx, MasterCard, Switch, Visa **DISCOUNTS** 10% unsplit case **DELIVERY** Free central London and Glos for 1 case or more; elsewhere 1 case £14, 2–3 cases £12.45 per case, 4 or more cases £10.15 per case, free orders over £650 **EN PRIMEUR** Bordeaux, Burgundy, Rhône. **G M T**
✪ Star attractions *HH&C's preference is for subtle, elegant wines, so you won't find too many hefty blockbusters here. It's most famous for Burgundy – but there are also lovely wines from the Loire, Alsace and Rhône, Germany, Spain, Australia, New Zealand and*

California. Bordeaux is chosen to suit every pocket. Their house Champagne, Pierre Vaudon, is invariably a winner.

Hedley Wright
11 Twyford Centre, London Road, Bishop's Stortford, Herts CM23 3YT (01279) 465818 **FAX** (01279) 465819 **E-MAIL** sales@hedleywright.co.uk **WEBSITE** www.hedleywright.co.uk **HOURS** Mon–Wed 9–6, Thur–Fri 9–7, Sat 10–6 **CARDS** AmEx, MasterCard, Switch, Visa **DELIVERY** £5 per delivery, free for orders over £100 **MINIMUM ORDER** 1 mixed case **EN PRIMEUR** Bordeaux, Chile, Germany, Port. **C G M T**
✪ Star attractions *A good all-round list that does justice to most French regions. Italy, something of a speciality, has wines from the likes of Pieropan, Allegrini and Le Pupille. Portugal, Spain, South Africa, New Zealand and Australia are packed with interesting wines, and Chile majors on the wines of Montes.*

Hicks & Don
4 Old Station Yard, Edington, Westbury, Wiltshire BA13 4NT (01380) 831234 **FAX** (01380) 831010 • Park House, North Elmham, Dereham, Norfolk NR20 5JY (01362) 668571 **FAX** (01362) 668573 **E-MAIL** mailbox@hicksanddon.co.uk **WEBSITE** www.hicksanddon.co.uk **HOURS** Mon–Fri 9–5 **CARDS** MasterCard, Switch, Visa **DISCOUNTS** Negotiable **DELIVERY** Free 3 cases or more UK mainland, otherwise £6 per case **MINIMUM ORDER** 1 case **EN PRIMEUR** Bordeaux, Burgundy, Chile, Italy, Port, Rhône. **C G M T**
✪ Star attractions *Subtle, well-made wines that go with food and plenty of good-value wines at around £6 for everyday drinking. The list is set out by style, regardless of origin: white Burgundies and other Chardonnays are followed by Sauvignons and Sémillons, then 'white wines of individuality' – the*

likes of Vin de Pays des Côtes de Gascogne, Muscadet and Pieropan's Soave Classico – then dessert wines, then Rieslings.

High Breck Vintners

MAIL ORDER 11 Nelson Road, London N8 9RX (020) 8340 1848 FAX (020) 8340 5162 E-MAIL hbv@richanl.freeserve.co.uk WEBSITE www.hbvwines.co.uk HOURS Mail order only; 24-hr answering machine for orders CARDS AmEx, MasterCard, Switch, Visa DELIVERY Free to the South-East, 3 or more cases; supplements payable for smaller orders or other locations MINIMUM ORDER 1 mixed case EN PRIMEUR Bordeaux.
C G M T

✪ Star attractions *A shortlist list with the focus on France. Madiran is from Alain Brumont, Sancerre from Gitton Père et Fils, and the red Bordeaux list looks interesting. Wines from lesser-known appellations like Costières de Nîmes can provide good drinking at lower prices.*

Jeroboams (incorporating Laytons and La Réserve)

HEAD OFFICE 43 Portland Road, London W11 4LJ (020) 7985 1560 FAX (020) 7229 1085 MAIL ORDER Jeroboams, 6 Pont Street, London SW1X 9EL (020) 7259 6716 FAX (020) 7235 7246 SHOPS 50–52 Elizabeth Street, London SW1W 9PB (020) 7730 8108 • 51 Elizabeth Street, London SW1W 9PP (020) 7823 5623
• 20 Davies Street, London W1K 3DT (020) 7499 1015
• 77–78 Chancery Lane, London WC2A 1AE (020) 7405 0552
• 96 Holland Park Avenue, London W11 3RB (020) 7727 9359
• 6 Pont Street, London SW1X 9EL (020) 7235 1612
• 29 Heath Street, London NW3 6TR (020) 7435 6845
• 56 Walton Street, London SW3 1RB (020) 7589 2020

• Mr Christian's Delicatessen, 11 Elgin Crescent, London W11 2JA (020) 7229 0501
• Milroy's of Soho, 3 Greek Street, London W1D 4NX (020) 7437 2385 E-MAIL sales@jeroboams.co.uk WEBSITES www.jeroboams.co.uk HOURS Offices Mon–Fri 9–6, shops Mon–Sat 9–7 (may vary) CARDS AmEx, MasterCard, Switch, Visa DELIVERY Shops: free for orders of £50 or over in central London; mail order free for orders over £200, otherwise £10 delivery charge EN PRIMEUR Bordeaux, Burgundy, Rhône. C G M T

✪ Star attractions *Sensibly priced everyday clarets as well as classed growths, interesting Burgundies and a good list from the Rhône. Other regions of France – including Jura – are covered though in less depth. Italy and Australia – in particular Western Australia – are new specialities. A wide range of fine foods, especially cheeses and olive oils, is available in the shops.*

S H Jones

27 High Street, Banbury, Oxfordshire OX16 5EW (01295) 251179 FAX (01295) 272352
• 9 Market Square, Bicester, Oxfordshire OX26 6AA (01869) 322448 • The Cellar Shop, 2 Riverside Tramway Road, Banbury, Oxfordshire OX16 5TU (01295) 251177 FAX (01295) 259560 • 121 Regent Street, Leamington Spa, Warwickshire CV32 4NU (01926) 315609 E-MAIL retail@shjones.com WEBSITE www.shjones.com HOURS Mon–Sat 8.30–6 CARDS MasterCard, Switch, Visa DELIVERY Free within van delivery area for 1 case or more; 'small charge' otherwise. Elsewhere £9.50; free for orders over £250 EN PRIMEUR Bordeaux, Burgundy, Port. C G M T

✪ Star attractions *Wide-ranging list: good Burgundies and Rhônes; some top-name clarets, along with 'everyday' ones at around £10; and* a comprehensive and affordable selection from southern France. Other good stuff from Old and New World includes Dr Loosen from Germany and Terrazas de los Andes from Argentina.

Justerini & Brooks

MAIL ORDER 61 St James's Street, London SW1A 1LZ (020) 7484 6400 **FAX** (020) 7484 6499 **E-MAIL** justorders@justerinis.com **WEBSITE** www.justerinis.com
HOURS Mon–Fri 9–5.30 **CARDS** AmEx, MasterCard, Switch, Visa **DELIVERY** Free for orders over £250, otherwise £15 UK mainland **MINIMUM ORDER** 1 case **EN PRIMEUR** Bordeaux, Burgundy, Italy, Rhône, Germany. **C G M T**
✪ Star attractions Superb list of top-quality wines from Europe's classic regions. The New World, though succinct, also has some excellent drinking. And while there are some very classy – and pricy – wines here, you'll find plenty of bottles under £8.50.

Kwiksave

See Somerfield.

Laithwaites

MAIL ORDER New Aquitaine House, Exeter Way, Theale, Reading, Berks RG7 4PL; **ORDER LINE** 0870 444 8383 **FAX** 0870 444 8182 **E-MAIL** orders@laithwaites.co.uk **WEBSITE** www.laithwaites.co.uk **HOURS** 24-hr answering machine **CARDS** AmEx, Diners, MasterCard, Switch, Visa **DISCOUNTS** On unmixed cases of 6 or 12 **DELIVERY** £4.99 per order **EN PRIMEUR** Australia, Bordeaux, Burgundy, Port, Rhône, Rioja. **C M T**
✪ Star attractions Good selection including well-known names and interesting finds. France represents around 50% of the list, but you may also find wines from Uruguay, Mexico or Moldova. The lists are generally the same as those for the

Sunday Times Wine Club although some wines are exclusive to each. User-friendly website offers excellent mixed cases, while the bin ends and special offers are good value. Added extras include wine plans offering regular delivery of hand-picked cases, and a comprehensive database for matching wine and food – from cold fresh prawns to kangaroo steaks!

The Lay & Wheeler Group

Holton Park, Holston St Mary, Suffolk, CO7 6NN 0845 330 1855 **FAX** 0845 30 4095 **E-MAIL** sales@laywheeler.com **WEBSITE** www.laywheeler.com **HOURS** (order office) Mon–Fri 8.30–5.30, Sat 9–1 **CARDS** AmEx, MasterCard, Switch, Visa **DELIVERY** £7.95; free for orders over £200 **EN PRIMEUR** Alsace, Australia, Bordeaux, Burgundy, California, Champagne, Germany, Italy, Loire, Rhône, Spain. **C G M T**
✪ Star attractions There's enough first-class Bordeaux and Burgundy to satisfy the most demanding drinker here; indeed everything is excellent. A must-have list – and if you really can't make up your mind, their mixed cases are excellent too.

Laymont & Shaw

The Old Chapel, Millpool, Truro, Cornwall TR1 1EX (01872) 270545 **FAX** (01872) 223005 **E-MAIL** info@laymont-shaw.co.uk **WEBSITE** www.laymont-shaw.co.uk **HOURS** Mon–Fri 9–5 **CARDS** MasterCard, Switch, Visa **DISCOUNTS** £5 per case if wines collected, also £1 per case for 2 cases, £2 for 3–5, £3 for 6 or more **DELIVERY** Free UK mainland **MINIMUM ORDER** 1 mixed case. **C G M T**
✪ Star attractions An excellent, knowledgeable list that specializes in Spain, with Portugal, Uruguay and Argentina also featuring. And

when I say 'specializes', I mean that they seek out wines that you won't find in supermarkets because the quantities are too small.

Laytons

See Jeroboams.

Lea & Sandeman

170 Fulham Road, London SW10 9PR (020) 7244 0522 **FAX** (020) 7244 0533 • 211 Kensington Church Street, London W8 7LX (020) 7221 1982 • 51 High Street, Barnes, London SW13 9LN (020) 8878 8643 **E-MAIL** info@leaandsandeman.co.uk **WEBSITE** www.londonfinewine.co.uk **HOURS** Mon–Sat 10–8 **CARDS** AmEx, MasterCard, Switch, Visa **DISCOUNTS** 5–15% by case, other discounts on 10 cases or more **DELIVERY** £5 for less than 1 case; free 1 case or more London, and to UK mainland south of Perth on orders over £250 **EN PRIMEUR** Bordeaux, Burgundy, Italy. **C G M T**
✪ **Star attractions** Burgundy and Italy take precedence here, and there's a succession of excellent names, chosen with great care. But L&S really do seek out unknown treasures wherever they go, so it's worth taking the time to study the list carefully. Bordeaux has wines at all price levels, and there are short but fascinating ranges from the USA, Spain, Australia's Mornington Peninsula and Central Otago in New Zealand. Lea and Sandeman are also the UK agents for Valdespino sherries.

Liberty Wines

MAIL ORDER Unit D18, New Covent Garden Food Market, London SW8 5LL (020) 7720 5350 **FAX** (020) 7720 6158 **E-MAIL** info@libertywine.co.uk **HOURS** Mon–Fri 9–5.30 **CARDS** MasterCard, Switch, Visa **DELIVERY** Free to mainland UK **MINIMUM ORDER** 1 mixed case. **M**
✪ **Star attractions** Italy rules, with superb wines and pretty well all the best producers from all over the country. Liberty are the UK agents for most of their producers, so if you're interested in Italian wines, this should be your first port of call. Australia features top producers such as Cullen, Mount Horrocks, Charles Melton and Plantagenet to name but a few. France, Germany, Austria, Spain, California and South America are not neglected.

Linlithgow Wines

Crossford, Station Road, Linlithgow, West Lothian EH49 6BW **TEL & FAX** (01506) 848821 **E-MAIL** jrobmcd@aol.com **HOURS** Mon–Fri 9–5.30 (please phone first) **CARDS** none: cash and cheque only **DELIVERY** Free locally; from £5 per case in UK. **G M T**
✪ **Star attractions** Specialist in the south of France – Languedoc, southern Rhône and Provence – with lots around £5; prices rarely exceed £20, unless you're tempted by top names such as Dom. de Trévallon and Châteauneuf-du-Pape from Dom. Font de Michelle. There's also a short list of Chablis and Champagne to offset all those sunny southern reds.

O W Loeb & Co

3 Archie Street, off Tanner Street, London SE1 3JT (020) 7234 0385 **FAX** (020) 7357 0440 **E-MAIL** brough@owloeb.com **WEBSITE** www.owloeb.com **HOURS** Mon–Fri 8.30–5.30 **CARDS** MasterCard, Switch, Visa **DISCOUNTS** 3 cases and above **DELIVERY** Free 3 cases or more **MINIMUM ORDER** 1 case **EN PRIMEUR** Burgundy, Bordeaux, Rhône, Germany (Mosel). **C M T**
✪ **Star attractions** Burgundy, the Rhône, Loire and Germany stand out, with top producers galore. Then there are Loeb's new discoveries from Spain and the New World, especially New Zealand and South Africa.

MAISON DU VIN

An exciting destination for the wine lover.

- Superb value wines from dozens of small quality growers
- Especially featuring wines of Château Coujan, Saint-Chinian Château Bassanel, Minervois Château Anglade, Faugères Domaine de Chantegut, Vacqueyras Domaine Le Souverain, Côtes du Rhône Villages Domaine Mucyn, Crozes-Hermitage

Rare vintages available for sale by the bottle

- Two fine wine auctions per year
- Monthly 'Meet the Growers' tastings at our Wine School
- UK/Overseas gift and mail order service
- Suppliers to trade and retail
- Wine tour organisers

Prime Wines Ltd
Maison du Vin, Moor Hill, Hawkhurst, Kent TN18 4PF
Tel: +44 1580 753487
Fax: +44 1580 755627
Email: info@maison-du-vin.co.uk

www.maison-du-vin.co.uk

Maison du Vin

Moor Hill, Hawkhurst, Kent TN18 4PF (01580) 753487 **FAX** (01580) 755627 **E-MAIL** kvgriffin@aol.com **WEBSITE** www.maison-du-vin.co.uk **HOURS** Mon, Tues, Thur, Fri 10–5, Sat 10–6, Sun 12–4 **CARDS** AmEx, Access, MasterCard, Switch, Visa **DELIVERY** Free locally; UK mainland at cost **EN PRIMEUR** Bordeaux.
C G M T
✪ **Star attractions** As the name suggests, the focus here is on French wine, at prices ranging from around £5 to £120 for a 1988 Ch. Latour. Also some thoughtfully chosen Italian wines. There's a monthly themed 'wine school' or you can book personal tutored tastings.

Majestic

(see also Wine and Beer World) **HEAD OFFICE** Majestic House, Otterspool Way, Watford, Herts WD25 8WW (01923) 298200 **FAX** (01923) 819105; 122 stores

nationwide **E-MAIL** info@majestic. co.uk **WEBSITE** www.majestic.co.uk **HOURS** Mon–Fri 10–8, Sat 9–7, Sun 10–5 (may vary) **CARDS** AmEx, Diners, MasterCard, Switch, Visa **DELIVERY** Free UK mainland **MINIMUM ORDER** 1 mixed case **EN PRIMEUR** Bordeaux, Port. **G M T**
✪ **Star attractions** This has long been one of the best places to come for Champagne, with a good range and good discounts for buying in quantity. Elsewhere you'll find real stars rubbing shoulders with some interesting oddballs. The Loire and Alsace are good, as are Germany, Italy and most of the New World.

Marks & Spencer

HEAD OFFICE Waterside House, 35 North Wharf Road, London, W2 1NW (020) 7935 4422 **FAX** (020) 7723 4924; 350 licensed stores **WEBSITE** www.marksandspencer.com **HOURS** Variable **DISCOUNTS** Variable, Wine of the Month, 12 bottles for the price of 11. **T**
✪ **Star attractions** M&S has clearly been beavering away in the New World vineyards of Australia and New Zealand, Chile and Argentina, seeking out top producers for their own-label wines. Their Spanish range is looking just as good this year as it did last year.

Martinez Wines

35 The Grove, Ilkley, Leeds, W. Yorks LS29 9NJ (01943) 600000 **FAX** 0870 922 3940 **E-MAIL** editor@martinez. co.uk **WEBSITE** www.martinez.co.uk **HOURS** Sun 1–6, Mon–Wed 10–8, Thurs–Fri 10–9, Sat 9.30–6 **CARDS** AmEx, MasterCard, Switch, Visa **DISCOUNTS** 5% on 6 bottles or more, 10% off orders over £150 **DELIVERY** Free local delivery, otherwise £13 per case mainland UK **EN PRIMEUR** Bordeaux, Burgundy. **C G M T**
✪ **Star attractions** Starting at the beginning, Alsace and Beaujolais look spot-on. Bordeaux, Burgundy

and Rhône are carefully chosen, and so I would trust their selections from other regions – sweeties and fortifieds are strong, too.

Mayfair Cellars

Unit 3b, Farm Lane Trading Centre, 101 Farm Lane, London SW6 1QJ (020) 7386 7999 FAX (020) 7386 0202 E-MAIL sales@mayfaircellars. co.uk WEBSITE www.mayfaircellars. co.uk HOURS Mon–Fri 9–6 CARDS AmEx, MasterCard, Switch, Visa DELIVERY England & Wales free; Scotland ring for details MINIMUM ORDER 1 mixed case EN PRIMEUR Bordeaux, Burgundy, Rhône. C M T
✪ Star attractions *Mail-order specialist in the classic regions of Europe, from first-rate small producers not available in the high street. There are also wines from California and Tasmania and a full range of Jacquesson Champagnes.*

Millésima

87 Quai de Paludate, BP 89, 33038 Bordeaux Cedex, France (00 33) 5 57 80 88 13 FAX (00 33) 5 57 80 88 19 Freephone 00800 26 73 32 89 or 0800 917 0352
WEBSITE www.millesima.com HOURS Mon–Fri 8–5.30 CARDS AmEx, Diners, MasterCard, Switch, Visa DELIVERY Free for orders over £500, otherwise £20 EN PRIMEUR Bordeaux, Burgundy, Rhône. C M T
✪ Star attractions *Wines come direct from the châteaux to Millésima's cellars, where 3 million bottles are stored. A sprinkling of established names from other French regions.*

Mills Whitcombe

New Lodge Farm, Peterchurch, Hereford HR3 6BJ (01981) 550028 FAX (01981) 550027 E-MAIL info@millswhitcombe.co.uk WEBSITE www.millswhitcombe.co.uk HOURS Mon–Fri 10–6, out-of-hours answering machine for orders

CARDS AmEx, MasterCard, Solo, Switch, Visa DISCOUNTS 5% for wine collected from warehouse DELIVERY Free locally, £7.50 per consignment nationwide, free for orders over £180 EN PRIMEUR Bordeaux, Burgundy. C G M T
✪ Star attractions *Young company with an expanding list of quality wines from a wide range of regions, especially Australia, Italy, Portugal, southern France and South Africa.*

Montrachet

MAIL ORDER 59 Kennington Road, London SE1 7PZ (020) 7928 1990 FAX (020) 7928 3415 E-MAIL charles@montrachetwine.com WEBSITE www.montrachetwine. com HOURS (Office and mail order) Mon–Fri 8.30–5.30 CARDS MasterCard, Switch, Visa DELIVERY England and Wales £12 including VAT, free for 3 or more cases; Scotland ring for details MINIMUM ORDER 1 unmixed case EN PRIMEUR Bordeaux, Burgundy. M T
✪ Star attractions *Impressive Burgundies, some very good Rhônes, and Bordeaux is excellent at all price levels. A short but starry set of German wines.*

Moreno Wines

11 Marylands Road, London W9 2DU (020) 7286 0678 FAX (020) 7286 0513 E-MAIL merchant@ moreno-wines.co.uk WEBSITE www.morenowinedirect.co.uk HOURS Mon–Fri 4–9, Sat 12–10 CARDS AmEx, MasterCard, Switch, Visa DISCOUNTS 5% 1 or 2 cases, 10% 3 or more cases DELIVERY Free locally. M
✪ Star attractions *Fine and rare Spanish wines, but plenty of everyday drinking too, from upcoming regions like Aragon and Castilla y León. Then there's weird and wonderful stuff like Txomin from the Basque country, or Don P X Gran Reserva, a wonderful Christmas pudding of a wine from*

Montilla-Moriles in the sunny south.
Also wines from South America.

Moriarty Vintners

19 Wyndham Arcade, Cardiff CF10
1RH (02920) 229996 FAX (02920)
664814 E-MAIL sales@moriarty-
vintners.com WEBSITE
www.moriarty-vintners.com
HOURS Mon–Sat 10–6 DISCOUNTS 5%
off 6 bottles; 10% off 1 mixed case
and regular special offers DELIVERY
free locally, nationwide at cost EN
PRIMEUR Italy, Port, Rhône. C G M T
✪ Star attractions *This growing list*
concentrates on exciting gems from
small producers. Italy is particularly
strong and other regions with good
coverage include the Languedoc,
Bordeaux, Australia and Spain.

Wm Morrison Supermarkets

HEAD OFFICE Hilmore House,
Thorton Road, Bradford, W. Yorks
BD8 9AX (01274) 494166
FAX (01274) 494831
CUSTOMER SERVICE (01274) 356000
130 licensed branches WEBSITE
www.morrisons.co.uk HOURS
Variable, generally Mon–Sat 8–8,
Sun 10–4 CARDS MasterCard,
Switch, Visa. G T, AmEx
✪ Star attractions *Inexpensive,*
often tasty wines. Southern France,
Chile and Argentina look
particularly reliable.

New Zealand Wines Direct

MAIL ORDER PO Box 476, London
NW5 2NZ (020) 7482 0093 FAX
(020) 7267 8400 E-MAIL sales@
fwnz.co.uk or info@fwnz.co.uk
WEBSITE www.fwnz.co.uk HOURS
Mon–Sat 9–6 CARDS MasterCard,
Visa DISCOUNTS 6 or more cases
DELIVERY Free for 1 mixed case or
more UK mainland MINIMUM ORDER
1 mixed case. M T
✪ Star attractions *Some great New*
Zealand wines: Ata Rangi, Hunter's,
Kumeu River, Pegasus Bay, Palliser
Estate, Quartz Reef, plus Bordeaux-
style Larose from Stonyridge.

James Nicholson

27A Killyleagh Street, Crossgar, Co.
Down, N Ireland BT30 9DQ (028)
4483 0091 FAX (028) 4483 0028
E-MAIL info@jnwine.com
and shop@jnwine.com WEBSITE
www.jnwine.com HOURS Mon–Sat
10–7 CARDS MasterCard, Switch,
Visa DISCOUNTS 10% mixed case
DELIVERY Free (1 case or more) in
Eire and N Ireland; UK mainland
£6.95 EN PRIMEUR Bordeaux,
Burgundy, California. G M T
✪ Star attractions *Everything is*
well chosen, mainly from small,
committed growers around the
world. Bordeaux, Rhône and
southern France are slightly ahead
of the field, and there's a good
selection of affordable Burgundy –
as affordable as decent Burgundy
ever is, anyway. Spain has new-wave
wines from the likes of Artadi and
Cellers de Capçanes, and there's
excellent drinking from Germany.

Nickolls & Perks

37 High Street, Stourbridge, West
Midlands DY8 1TA (01384) 394518
FAX (01384) 440786 E-MAIL sales@
nickollsandperks.co.uk WEBSITE
www.nickollsandperks.co.uk
HOURS Mon–Fri 9.30–6, Sat 10–5
CARDS MasterCard, Switch, Visa
DISCOUNTS negotiable DELIVERY £10
per consignment MINIMUM ORDER
1 mixed case. EN PRIMEUR Bordeaux,
Port. C G M T
✪ Star attractions *Wine shippers*
since 1797, Nickolls & Perks has
always been important in the en
primeur Bordeaux market. The wide-
ranging list – and terrific website –
covers most areas and is particularly
strong in France. Advice is available
to clients wishing to develop their
cellars or invest in wine.

Nidderdale Fine Wines

2a High Street, Pateley Bridge,
North Yorkshire HG3 5AW
(01423) 711703 E-MAIL
info@southaustralianwines.com

WEBSITE
www.southaustralianwines.com
HOURS Tue–Fri 10–7, Sat 9–5.30, Sun
10–5.30 CARDS MasterCard, Switch,
Visa DISCOUNTS 5% case discount
on shop purchases DELIVERY £5 per
case in England, Wales and
southern Scotland; rest of UK £25
per case. Single bottle delivery
negotiable. G T
✪ Star attractions *South Australia is
the speciality here, with 400 wines
broken down into regions, so if you
want to see what's available from
Barossa, Coonawarra, Adelaide Hills
or Clare Valley, you need look no
further. Also 350 or so wines from
other parts of Australia and the rest
of the world. Look out for online
offers and winemaker dinners.*

Noble Rot Wine Warehouses

18 Market Street, Bromsgrove,
Worcestershire, B61 8DA
(01527) 575606 FAX (01527) 833133
E-MAIL info@noble-rot.co.uk
WEBSITE www.noble-rot.co.uk
HOURS Mon–Fri 10–7, Sat 9.30–6.30
CARDS MasterCard, Switch, Visa
DISCOUNTS Various DELIVERY Free
within 10 mile radius. G T
✪ Star attractions *What Noble Rot's
customers want is good wine for
current drinking, mostly at £4 to £15
a bottle. Australia, Italy, France and
Spain feature most strongly in a
frequently changing list of more
than 400 wines.*

The Nobody Inn

Doddiscombsleigh, Nr Exeter,
Devon EX6 7PS (01647) 252394
FAX (01647) 252978 E-MAIL
info@nobodyinn.co.uk
WEBSITE www.nobodyinn.co.uk
HOURS Mon–Sat 12–2.30 & 6–11
(summer); 6–11 (winter), Sun 12–3
& 7–10.30; or by appointment
CARDS AmEx, MasterCard, Switch,
Visa DISCOUNTS 5% per case
DELIVERY £7.99 for 1 case, free over
£150. G M T
• The Wine Company (01392)

477752 FAX (01392) 477759 E-MAIL
sales@thewinecompany.biz
WEBSITE www.thewinecompany.biz
HOURS Mon–Fri 9.30–6, 24-hr
ordering service CARDS AmEx,
MasterCard, Switch, Visa DELIVERY
Free for orders over £150.
✪ Star attractions *If you're going to
eat here I advise you to turn up 2
hours early to browse through this
extraordinary list. Australia rules,
but there's something exciting from
just about everywhere. Amazing
range of sweet wines: Loire, of
course, but also Greece's Samos
Muscat and Anthemis. The Wine
Company is a mail order venture for
wines mostly priced at £5–10.*

Oddbins

HEAD OFFICE 31–33 Weir Road,
London SW19 8UG (020) 8944
4400 FAX (020) 8944 4411
MAIL ORDER Oddbins Direct 0800
328 2323 FAX 0800 328 3848;
227 shops nationwide
WEBSITE www.oddbins.com
HOURS Ask local branch for details
CARDS AmEx, MasterCard, Switch,
Visa DISCOUNTS regular offers on
Champagne and sparkling wine,
and general promotions DELIVERY
(Stores) free locally for orders over
£100 EN PRIMEUR Bordeaux. G M T
• CALAIS STORE Cité Europe, 139 Rue
de Douvres, 62901, Coquelles
Cedex, France (0033) 3 21 82 07 32
FAX (0033) 3 21 82 05 83 PRE-ORDER
www.oddbins.com/
storefinder/calais.asp
✪ Star attractions *New World
pioneer or champion of the classics?
Both, actually. Extensive Aussie
selection, well-chosen Chileans and
Argentinians; Spain, Italy, Greece,
New Zealand, South Africa,
Burgundy and Rhône all look good,
and Languedoc is currently in the
limelight. Great deals on
Champagne. Now owned by French
multinational group Castel who are
also owners of the Nicolas chain of
wine shops.*

OZ WINES • OZ WINES • OZ WINES

OZ WINES

RICHLY CONCENTRATED WINES MADE BY REAL PEOPLE.

'Australian wines made by small wineries and real people. This is what the true Australia is all about – not big brands deeply discounted on a supermarket shelf'.
Oz Clarke

Create your own mixed case of twelve wines or more from our celebrated, award-winning list of superb Aussie wines. Alternatively, take advantage of some exciting pre-mixed cases.

ALL FOR FREE DELIVERY TO YOUR DOOR WITHIN 5 DAYS.

OZ WINES
Tel: 0845 450 1261
Fax: 020 8870 8839
Email: info@ozwines.co.uk
www.ozwines.co.uk

Oz Wines

MAIL ORDER Freepost Lon 17656, London SW18 5BR, 0845 450 1261 FAX (020) 8870 8839 E-MAIL sales@ozwines.co.uk WEBSITE www.ozwines.co.uk HOURS Mon–Fri 9.30–7 CARDS Diners, MasterCard, Switch, Visa DELIVERY Free. MINIMUM ORDER 1 mixed case. **M**
✪ Star attractions *Australian wines made by small wineries and real wines, which means wines with the kind of thrilling flavours that Australians do better than anyone else.*

Penistone Court Wine Cellars

The Railway Station, Penistone, Sheffield, South Yorkshire S36 6HP (01226) 766037 FAX (01226) 767310 E-MAIL chris@pcwine.plus.com

HOURS Tues–Fri 10–6, Sat 10–3 CARDS MasterCard, Switch, Visa DELIVERY Free locally, rest of UK mainland charged at cost 1 case or more MINIMUM ORDER 1 case. **G M**
✪ Star attractions *A well-balanced list, with something from just about everywhere, mostly from familiar names. So, you've got Champagne (Pol Roger, Bollinger, Roederer and others), Burgundy, Beaujolais, Alsace, Loire, Rhône and a short list of clarets. Outside France, there's a good range from Italy, plus Austria, Spain, Chile, the USA, New Zealand and Australia (Brown Brothers, Stonier, Penfolds, De Bortoli).*

Philglas & Swiggot

21 Northcote Road, Battersea, London SW11 1NG (020) 7924 4494 • 64 Hill Rise, Richmond, London TW10 6UB (020) 8332 6081 E-MAIL info@philglas-swiggot.co.uk WEBSITE www.philglas-swiggot.co.uk HOURS (Battersea) Mon–Sat 11–7, Sun 12–5 (Richmond) Tue–Sat 11–7, Sun 12–5 CARDS AmEx, MasterCard, Switch, Visa DISCOUNTS 5% per case DELIVERY Free 1 case locally. **G M T**
✪ Star attractions *Excellent Aussie selection – subtle, interesting wines, not blockbuster brands. The same philosophy applies to wines they buy from elsewhere, so you'll find serious Italians and good French wines. Austria fits the bill nicely and dessert wines are good too.*

Christopher Piper Wines

1 Silver Street, Ottery St Mary, Devon EX11 1DB (01404) 814139 FAX (01404) 812100 E-MAIL sales@christopherpiperwines.co.uk WEBSITE www.christopherpiperwines.co.uk HOURS Mon–Fri 8.30–5.30, Sat 9–4.30 CARDS MasterCard, Switch, Visa DISCOUNTS 5% mixed case, 10% 3 or more cases DELIVERY Free for orders over £190, otherwise £7.05 per case MINIMUM ORDER (for mail

order) 1 mixed case **EN PREMIEUR**
Bordeaux, Burgundy, Rhône. **C G M T**
✪ **Star attractions** *Huge range of
well-chosen wines that reflect a
sense of place and personality, with
lots of information to help you
make up your mind. The shop is
open 6 days a week for single
bottle sales.*

Terry Platt Wine Merchants

Council Street West, Llandudno
LL30 1ED (01492) 874099 **FAX**
(01492) 874788 **E-MAIL** info@
terryplattwines.co.uk **WEBSITE**
www.terryplattwines.co.uk
HOURS Mon–Fri 8.30–5.30 **CARDS**
Access, MasterCard, Switch, Visa
DELIVERY Free locally and UK
mainland 5 cases or more
MINIMUM ORDER 1 mixed case.
G M T
✪ **Star attractions** *A wide-ranging
list with a sprinkling of good
growers from most regions. New
World coverage has increased
recently: Terrazas de los Andes from
Argentina; Casa Lapostolle and
Montes from Chile; Grangehurst
and Warwick Estate from South
Africa; Water Wheel and Cape
Mentelle from Australia.*

Playford Ros

Middle Park, Thirsk, Yorkshire YO7
3AH (01845) 526777 **FAX** (01845)
526888 **E-MAIL**
sales@playfordros.com
WEBSITE www.playfordros.com
HOURS Mon–Fri 8–6 **CARDS**
MasterCard, Visa **DISCOUNTS**
negotiable **DELIVERY** Free Yorkshire,
Derbyshire, Durham, Newcastle;
elsewhere on UK mainland (per
case), £15 1 case, £8.50 2 cases,
£7 3 cases, £6.50 4 cases, £5 5 cases
MINIMUM ORDER 1 mixed case
EN PREMIEUR Bordeaux, Burgundy.
C G M T
✪ **Star attractions** *A carefully
chosen list, with reassuring
recognizable representatives from
Bordeaux and Burgundy, the Rhône*

*and the Loire. Similar standards
apply elsewhere, with Australia
looking exceptional, and there is a
good selection of wines at around
the £5 to £6 mark.*

Portland Wine Co

16 North Parade, off Norris Road,
Sale, Cheshire M33 3JS (0161) 962
8752 **FAX** (0161) 905 1291 • 152a
Ashley Road, Hale WA15 9SA (0161)
928 0357 • 82 Chester Road,
Macclesfield SK11 8DL (01625)
616147 **E-MAIL** enquiries@
portlandwine.co.uk **WEBSITE**
www.portlandwine.co.uk
HOURS Mon–Sat 10–10, Sun 12–9.30
CARDS MasterCard, Switch, Visa
DISCOUNTS 5% 2 cases or more, 10%
5 cases or more **DELIVERY** Free
locally 1 case or more, £10 + VAT
per consignment nationwide
EN PREMIEUR Bordeaux. **C T**
✪ **Star attractions** *Spain, Portugal
and Burgundy are specialities;there
is also a promising-looking list of
lesser clarets, as well as more
expensive, stunning older vintages.
This consumer-friendly list has
something at every price level from
around the world.*

Raeburn Fine Wines

21–23 Comely Bank Road,
Edinburgh EH4 1DS (0131) 343 1159
FAX (0131) 332 5166 **E-MAIL**
sales@raeburnfinewines.com
WEBSITE www.raeburnfine
wines.com **HOURS** Mon–Sat
9.30–6, Sun 12.30–5 **CARDS** AmEx,
MasterCard, Switch, Visa **DISCOUNTS**
5% unsplit case, 2.5% mixed
DELIVERY Free local area 1 or more
cases (usually); elsewhere at cost
EN PREMIEUR Australia, Bordeaux,
Burgundy, California, Germany,
Italy, Languedoc-Roussillon, Loire,
New Zealand, Rhône. **G M T**
✪ **Star attractions** *Everything here
is carefully chosen, usually from
small growers: if you want obvious
choices you won't like this list, but if
you want to try interesting wines*

from an impressive array of
vintages you'll be more than happy.
Burgundy is something of a
speciality and from the Loire there
are oodles of Vouvrays from Huet, in
vintages going back to 1924. Italy,
North Spain and California all look
fabulous. Ports from Niepoort.

Reid Wines

The Mill, Marsh Lane, Hallatrow,
Nr Bristol BS39 6EB (01761) 452645
FAX (01761) 453642 **HOURS** Mon–Fri
9–5.30 **CARDS** MasterCard, Visa (3%
charge) **DELIVERY** Free within 25
miles of Hallatrow (Bristol), and in
central London for orders over 2
cases **C G M T**
✪ **Star attractions** Reid's is one of
the lists I look forward to reading
most: it's full of pithy comments
alongside its fabulous array of older
vintages. Five clarets from 1975 were
'heralded at birth, scorned in middle
age, graceful and delicious (some of
them) now.' A mix of great old
wines, some old duds and splendid
current stuff. Italy, USA, Australia,
port and Madeira look tremendous.

Richardson & Sons

26a Lowther Street, Whitehaven,
Cumbria CA28 7DG **FAX/TEL** (01946)
65334 **E-MAIL** mailwines@aol.com
HOURS Mon–Sat 10–5.30 **CARDS**
AmEx, Delta, MasterCard, Switch,
Visa **DELIVERY** Free locally **G M T**
✪ **Star attractions** It's the only
place in Cumbria stocking Ch.
Latour and Opus One, but in
general Richardson & Sons carefully
select from interesting small
producers, preferring 'little hidden
gems' to big-name brands. Rioja is
chosen to represent various styles,
and there's some good stuff from
South Africa.

Howard Ripley

25 Dingwall Road, London
SW18 3AZ (020) 8877 3065
FAX (020) 8877 0029 **E-MAIL**
info@howardripley.com

WEBSITE www.howardripley.com
HOURS Mon–Fri 9–8, Sat 9–1
CARDS MasterCard, Switch, Visa
DELIVERY Minimum charge £10.50 +
VAT, free UK mainland on orders
over £500 ex-VAT **MINIMUM ORDER** 1
mixed case **EN PRIMEUR** Burgundy,
Germany. **C M T**
✪ **Star attractions** If you're serious
about Burgundy, this is one of
perhaps half a dozen lists that you
need. Yes, the wines are expensive –
great Burgundy is expensive – but
they're not excessive. The German
range is also excellent.

Roberson

348 Kensington High Street,
London W14 8NS (020) 7371 2121
FAX (020) 7371 4010
E-MAIL retail@roberson.co.uk
WEBSITE
www.robersonwinemerchant.co.uk
HOURS Mon–Sat 10–8 **CARDS** AmEx,
MasterCard, Switch, Visa **DISCOUNTS**
MAIL ORDER 5% on champagne and
spirits, 10% or wine cases **DELIVERY**
Free delivery within London,
otherwise £15 per case **EN PRIMEUR**
Bordeaux, Burgundy, Port. **C G M T**
✪ **Star attractions** Fine and rare
wines, sold by the bottle. Plenty of
clarets from the great 1989 and
1990 vintages. All of France is
excellent; so is Italy and port.

The RSJ Wine Company

33 Coin Street, London SE1 9NR
(020) 7928 4554 **E-MAIL**
tom.king@rsj.uk.com
WEBSITE www.rsj.uk.com
HOURS Mon–Fri 9–6, answering
machine at other times **CARDS**
MasterCard, Switch, Amex, Visa
DELIVERY Free central London,
minimum 1 case; England and
Wales (per case), £14.10 1 case,
£10.25 2 cases or more. **G M T**
✪ **Star attractions** A roll-call of
great Loire names. From Savennières
there is Domaine aux Moines, from
Chinon J & C Baudry, from Saumur
Domaine des Roches Neuves, to

mention just a few. And now there are wines from outside the Loire as well: Beaujolais, Alsace, Italy, Australia and New Zealand.

Safeway

Now owned by Wm Morrison plc (see page 129)

Sainsbury's

HEAD OFFICE 33 Holborn, London EC1N 2HT (020) 7695 6000 CUSTOMER SERVICE 0800 636262; 720 stores WEBSITE www. sainsburys.co.uk HOURS Variable, some 24 hrs, locals generally Mon–Sat 7–11, Sun 10 or 11–4 CARDS AmEx, MasterCard, Switch, Visa DISCOUNTS 5% for 6 bottles or more **G M T · MAIL ORDER** 0800 917 4092 FAX 0800 917 4095 · CALAIS STORE Sainsbury's, Centre Commercial Auchan, Route de Boulogne, 62100 Calais, France (0033) 3 21 82 38 48 FAX (0033) 3 21 36 01 91 PREORDER www.sainsburys.co.uk/calais ✪ Star attractions *Sainsbury's manages to cater for bargain hunters as well as appealing to lovers of good-value wine higher up the scale. Very strong in Chile, and there's a short list of affordable clarets, a good range of fortified wines, and a willingness to venture into innovative areas.*

Savage Selection

The Ox House, Market Place, Northleach, Cheltenham, Glos GL54 3EG (01451) 860896 FAX (01451) 860996 · The Ox House Shop and Wine Bar at same address (01451) 860680 E-MAIL wine@savage selection.co.uk WEBSITE www.savageselection.co.uk HOURS Office: Mon–Fri 9–6; shop: Tue/Wed 10–7.30, Thur–Fri 10–10, Sat 10–3 CARDS AmEx, MasterCard, Switch, Visa DELIVERY Free locally for orders over £100; elsewhere on UK mainland free for orders over £250: otherwise £11.75 per

consignment EN PRIMEUR Bordeaux. **C G M T** ✪ Star attractions *If ever you find yourself getting bored by standard wine fare and feel the need for a seachange of flavours, get in touch with Mark Savage. He takes the trouble to find wines for himself, seeking them out in Austria, Hungary, Greece and Idaho as well as Italy, Spain and Germany. France is also strong, with wines from Bordeaux, Burgundy and Provence, and Billecart-Salmon Champagne.*

Seckford Wines

Dock Lane, Melton, Suffolk IP12 1PE (01394) 446622 FAX (01394) 446633 E-MAIL sales@seckfordwines.co.uk WEBSITE www.seckfordwines.co.uk CARDS MasterCard, Switch, Visa DELIVERY £10 per consignment, UK mainland; elsewhere at cost. MINIMUM ORDER 1 mixed case EN PRIMEUR Bordeaux, Burgundy. **C** ✪ Star attractions *Bordeaux, Burgundy and the Rhône are the stars of this list, and if you prefer older vintages, Seckford have got plenty of these. There's serious stuff from Italy, Spain and Austria, too.*

Somerfield

HEAD OFFICE Somerfield House, Whitchurch Lane, Bristol BS14 0TJ (0117) 935 9359 FAX (0117) 935 6669; 800 Somerfield stores and 500 Kwiksave stores nationwide WEBSITE www.somerfield.co.uk HOURS Mon–Sat 8–8, Sun 10–4 CARDS MasterCard, Switch, Visa DISCOUNTS 5% off 6 bottles DELIVERY Free local delivery for orders over £25 in selected stores **M T** ✪ Star attractions *Somerfield are relaunching their wine range in September with 200 new lines and increasing the range of New World, sparkling and rosé wines.*

Sommelier Wine Co

23 St George's Esplanade, St Peter Port, Guernsey, Channel Islands,

GY1 2BG (01481) 721677 **FAX** (01481) 716818 **HOURS** Mon–Sat 9.30–5.30 **CARDS** MasterCard, Switch, Visa **DISCOUNTS** 5% 1 case or more **DELIVERY** Free locally 1 unmixed case. Customs legislation restricts the shipping of wine to the UK mainland. **G T**

✪ Star attractions *An excellent list, with interesting, unusual wines. It's a big selection, too: there are yards of lovely subtle Italian whites and well-made reds, and lots of Loires and Beaujolais. Burgundy, Bordeaux, the Rhône, Spain, Italy and South Africa all look good, though Australia outdoes them all.*

Frank Stainton Wines

3 Berry's Yard, Finkle Street, Kendal, Cumbria LA9 4AB (01539) 731886 **FAX** (01539) 730396 **E-MAIL** admin@stainton-wines.co.uk **WEBSITE** www.stainton-wines.co.uk **HOURS** Mon–Sat 9–5.30 **CARDS** MasterCard, Switch, Visa **DISCOUNTS** 5% mixed case **DELIVERY** Free Cumbria and North Lancashire; elsewhere (per case) £12 1 case, £6 2–4 cases, £4 5–9 cases, 10 cases free. **G M T**

✪ Star attractions *Some interesting Burgundy growers, but on the whole Bordeaux is better. The worldwide range includes leading names from Italy and from Chile the wines of Casa Silva, which have real character and subtlety. Also Three Choirs wines from England.*

Stevens Garnier

47 West Way, Botley, Oxford OX2 0JF (01865) 263303 **FAX** (01865) 791594 **E-MAIL** shop@stevens garnier.co.uk **HOURS** Mon–Wed 10–6, Thur–Fri 10–7, Sat 9.30–6 **CARDS** AmEx, MasterCard, Switch, Visa, Solo **DISCOUNTS** 5% on a mixed case **DELIVERY** Free locally; 'competitive rates' elsewhere. **G T**

✪ Star attractions *'Regional France' is a strength: this is one of the few places in the UK you can buy wine*

from Savoie. Portugal is from quality-conscious Sogrape. Pleasant surprises from the New World include Grant Burge and Willow Bridge from Australia, Carmen from Chile and Chateau des Charmes from Canada.

Stone, Vine & Sun

No. 13 Humphrey Farms, Hazeley Road, Twyford, Winchester SO21 1QA 0845 061 4604 **FAX** (01962) 717545 **E-MAIL** sales@stonevine.co.uk **WEBSITE** www.stonevine.co.uk **HOURS** Mon–Fri 9–6, Sat 9.30–4 **CARDS** MasterCard, Switch, Visa **DISCOUNTS** 5% on an unmixed case **DELIVERY** £3.50 per case. Prices vary for Scottish highlands and islands and N Ireland. Free delivery for orders over £250 **G M T**

✪ Star attractions *Lovely list marked by enthusiasm and passion for the subject. Lots of interesting stuff from France, but also from Germany, South Africa, New Zealand and elsewhere – and they're determined to do it properly: whenever I'm nosing about the byways and backroads of France, who do I meet but someone from Stone, Vine & Sun doing the same thing?*

Sunday Times Wine Club

New Aquitaine House, Exeter Way, Theale, Reading, Berks RG7 4PL **ORDER LINE** 0870 220 0010 **FAX** 0870 220 0030 **E-MAIL** orders@sundaytimeswineclub.co.uk **WEBSITE** www.sundaytimeswine club.co.uk **HOURS** 24-hr answering machine **CARDS** AmEx, Diners, MasterCard, Switch, Visa **DELIVERY** £4.99 per order **EN PRIMEUR** Australia, Bordeaux, Burgundy, Rhône. **C M T**

✪ Star attractions *Essentially the same list as Laithwaites (see page 124), though the special offers come round at different times. The membership fee is £10 per annum. The club runs tours and tasting events for its members.*

T & W Wines

5 Station Way, Brandon, Suffolk IP27 0BH (01842) 814414 **FAX** (01842) 819967 **E-MAIL** contact@tw-wines.com **WEBSITE** www.tw-wines.com **HOURS** Mon–Fri. 9.30–5.30, occasional Sat 9.30–1 **CARDS** AmEx, MasterCard, Visa **DELIVERY** (most areas) 7–23 bottles £14.95 + VAT, 2 or more cases free **EN PRIMEUR** Burgundy. **C G M T**
✪ **Star attractions** *The list is a good one, particularly if you're looking for Burgundy, Rhône, Alsace or the Loire, but prices are not especially low, and when working out the final cost remember that they exclude VAT. There's an amazing list of over 240 half bottles, including the superb sweet wines of Willi Opitz, from Austria, and 25 biodynamic wines from France.*

Tanners

26 Wyle Cop, Shrewsbury, Shropshire SY1 1XD (01743) 234500 **FAX** (01743) 234501 • 4 St Peter's Square, Hereford HR1 2PG (01432) 272044 **FAX** (01432) 263316 • 36 High Street, Bridgnorth WV16 4DB (01746) 763148 **FAX** (01746) 769798 • Severn Farm Enterprise Park, Welshpool SY21 7DF (01938) 552542 **FAX** (01938) 556565 **E-MAIL** sales@tanners-wines.co.uk **WEBSITE** www.tanners-wines.co.uk **HOURS** Shrewsbury Mon–Sat 9–6, branches 9–5.30 **CARDS** AmEx, MasterCard, Switch, Visa **DISCOUNTS** 5% 1 mixed case (cash & collection); 2.5% for 3 mixed cases, 5% for 5, 7.5% for 10 (**MAIL ORDER**) **DELIVERY** Free 1 mixed case or more locally, or nationally over £80, otherwise £7.50 **MINIMUM ORDER** £25 **EN PRIMEUR** Bordeaux, Burgundy, Rhône, Germany, Port. **C G M T**
✪ **Star attractions** *The sort of list from which it's extremely difficult to choose, because you simply want everything on it. There are lots of lovely Rhônes; Bordeaux and Burgundy are both terrific; Germany is outstanding, and there are even a couple of wines from Switzerland, Greece and Lebanon. Spain and Italy look very good, and Australia, South Africa, Chile, Argentina and California all show what these places can do.*

Tesco

HEAD OFFICE Tesco House, PO Box 18, Delamare Road, Cheshunt EN8 9SL (01992) 632222 **FAX** (01992) 630794, **CUSTOMER SERVICE** 0800 505555; 916 licensed branches **E-MAIL** customer.services@tesco.co.uk **WEBSITE** www.tesco.co.uk **HOURS** Variable **CARDS** MasterCard, Switch, Visa **DISCOUNT** 5% on 6 bottles or more **G M T**
• **CALAIS STORE** Tesco Vin Plus, Cité Europe, 122 Boulevard du Kent, 62231 Coquelles, France (0033) 3 21 46 02 70 **WEBSITE** www.tesco.com/vinplus; www.tesco-france.com **HOURS** Mon–Sat 8.30–10pm
✪ **Star attractions** *This is looking increasingly like a place to do some serious wine shopping – the Tesco Finest range can reveal some true beauties, well worth the extra quid or two they'll cost. And there are still lots of cheapies for when your budget is more of the baked beans on toast sort.*

Thresher Group: Thresher Wine Shops and Wine Rack

HEAD OFFICE Enjoyment Hall, Bessemer Road, Welwyn Garden City, Herts AL7 1BL (01707) 387200 **FAX** (01707) 387350 **WEBSITE** www.threshergroup.com; 800 Thresher Wine Shops, 200 Wine Rack stores **HOURS** Mon–Sat 10–10 (some 10.30), Sun 11–10, Scotland 12.30–10.30 **CARDS** MasterCard, Switch, Visa **DELIVERY** Free locally, some branches. **G T**
✪ **Star attractions** *A major high street presence, Thresher wine shops are presumably a reflection of everyday wine drinking in Britain:*

there's certainly a good choice of Sauvignon Blanc. A lot of effort has gone into sourcing new wines over the past year: Australia and France take the leading roles, with strong support from New Zealand and Spain; some new and exciting stuff from South America is on the cards. Prices start at £3.99, but the 'buy any 2 bottles get the third bottle free' deal brings this down to £2.66 – it needn't be 3 of the same wine.

True Taste of Italy

The True Taste of Italy, Unit 8, Stretton Business Park, Brunel Drive, Stretton, Burton upon Trent, DE13 0BY (01283) 741976 **FAX** *(01283)* 741975 **E-MAIL** sales@thetruetasteofitaly.co.uk **WEBSITE** www.thetruetasteofitaly. co.uk **HOURS** Mon–Fri 9–5 **CARDS** Mastercard, Switch, Visa **DELIVERY** £4.99 **MINIMUM ORDER** Single bottles on specified wines, otherwise half or full case. **M T**
✪ **Star attractions** *Tuscany is a speciality, but the website offers a vinous tour of Italy – and the prices are reasonable.*

Turville Valley Wines

The Firs, Potter Row, Great Missenden, Bucks HP16 9LT (01494) 868818 **FAX** (01494) 868832 **E-MAIL** chris@turville-valley-wines.com **WEBSITE** www.turville-valley-wines.com **HOURS** Mon–Fri 9–5.30 **CARDS** None **DELIVERY** By arrangement **MINIMUM ORDER** £300/12 bottles. **C M**
✪ **Star attractions** *Serious wines for serious spenders. The Bordeaux is all classic, mostly mature stuff – no lesser wines here – and there are buckets of Domaine de la Romanée-Conti Burgundies. There are top names too from Spain, Italy, the Rhône, California (Screaming Eagle, Harlan Estate, Pahlmeyer), Australia (Grange, Duck Muck, Torbreck) and odds and ends from all over.*

Unwins

HEAD OFFICE Birchwood House, Victoria Road, Dartford, Kent DA1 5AJ (01322) 272711 **FAX** (01322) 294469; 383 branches in southern and eastern England **E-MAIL** info@unwins.co.uk **WEBSITE** www.unwins.co.uk **HOURS** Variable, usually Mon–Sat 10–10, Sun 11–10 **CARDS** AmEx, Diners, MasterCard, Switch, Visa **DISCOUNTS** 10% on mixed case, 5% on 6 bottles and regular special offers **DELIVERY** Free for orders over £100 **G T**
✪ **Star attractions** *The focus is on France, but the New World, especially Australia, is not forgotten. You're sure to find something if you're looking in the £5–10 range, but there's a fair bit under £5. The better Unwins shops have a fine wine selection, so if you're interested in good Bordeaux and Burgundy at a decent price, ask to see the list.*

Valvona & Crolla

19 Elm Row, Edinburgh EH7 4AA (0131) 556 6066 **FAX** (0131) 556 1668 **E-MAIL** wine@valvonacrolla.co.uk **WEBSITE** www.valvonacrolla.com **HOURS** Mon–Sat 8–6.30, Sun 11–5 **CARDS** AmEx, MasterCard, Switch, Visa **DISCOUNTS** 7% 1–3 cases, 10% 4 or more **DELIVERY** Free on orders over £125, £6 otherwise for 8 day service, £8 for next day service. **G M T**
✪ **Star attractions** *If you're fond of Italian wines you should be shopping here. The list has dozens and dozens of wines from Piedmont and Tuscany, and there are others from Lombardy, Basilicata, Calabria, the Marche, Sicily, Sardinia, the Veneto, and terrific dessert wines. It's a simply fabulous selection, and at all prices. There are wines from Australia, New Zealand, France, Argentina, Spain and Portugal and elsewhere, but they are not what V&C is really about.*

Villeneuve Wines

1 Venlaw Court, Peebles, Scotland
EH45 8AE (01721) 722500 **FAX**
(01721) 729922 • 82 High Street,
Haddington EH41 3ET (01620)
822224 • 49A Broughton Street,
Edinburgh EH1 3RJ (0131) 558 8441
E-MAIL
wines@villeneuvewines.com
WEBSITE
www.villeneuvewines.com
HOURS (Peebles) Mon–Sat 9–8, Sun
12.30-5.30 (Haddington) Mon–
Thur 10–7, Fri 10–8, Sat 9–8;
(Edinburgh) Mon–Sat 9–10, Sun 1-
8 **CARDS** AmEx, MasterCard,
Switch, Visa **DISCOUNTS** 5% per
case **DELIVERY** 48-hour service.
Free locally, £7.50 per case
elsewhere. **G M T**
✪ **Star attractions** *Italy, California,
Australia and New Zealand are all
marvellous here. Italy has
Pieropan, Planeta, Aldo Conterno,
Aldo Vajra, Isole e Olena, Jermann,
Allegrini and many others. From
California there are wines from
Duckhorn, Shafer, Stag's Leap, Ridge
and Joseph Phelps. Australia
includes Brokenwood, Mount Langi
Ghiran and Plantagenet and New
Zealand has Mount Difficulty,
Cloudy Bay and Felton Road. Spain
is clearly an enthusiasm.*

Vinceremos

74 Kirkgate, Leeds LS2 7DJ (0113)
244 0002 **FAX** (0113) 288 4566
E-MAIL info@vinceremos.co.uk
WEBSITE www.vinceremos.co.uk
HOURS Mon–Fri 8.30–5.30
CARDS AmEx, Delta, MasterCard,
Switch, Visa, **DISCOUNTS** 5% on 5
cases or over, 10% on 10 cases or
over **DELIVERY** Free delivery on £5
and over orders, free 5 cases or
more **MINIMUM ORDER** 1 mixed
case **M**
✪ **Star attractions** *Organic
specialist, with a wide-ranging list
of wines: Guy Bossard's Muscadet,
Huet's Vouvray, Sedlescombe in
England, Millton in New Zealand,*

*Fetzer's Bonterra wines from
California and a whole page of reds
and whites from Morocco.*

Vin du Van

MAIL ORDER Colthups, The Street,
Appledore, Kent TN26 2BX (01233)
758727 **FAX** (01233) 758389 **HOURS**
Mon–Fri 9–5 **CARDS** Delta,
MasterCard, Switch, Visa **DELIVERY**
Free locally; elsewhere £5.95 for
first case, further cases free.
Highlands & islands ask for quote
MINIMUM ORDER 1 case. **G M**
✪ **Star attractions** *Quirky, star-
studded Australian list, the kind of
inspired lunacy I'd take to read on
the first manned space trip to
Mars.*

Vintage Roots

Farley Farms, Reading Road,
Arborfield, Berkshire, RG2 9HT
(0118) 976 1999 **FAX** (0118) 976
1998 **HOURS** Mon–Fri 8.30–5.30,
Saturdays in December
E-MAIL info@vintageroots.co.uk
WEBSITE www.vintageroots.co.uk
CARDS Delta, MasterCard, Switch,
Visa **DISCOUNTS** 5% on 5 cases or
over **DELIVERY** £5.95 for single case,
£6.95 2–5 cases, free 6 cases or
more. **T**
✪ **Star attractions** *Everything on
this list is organic and/or
biodynamic, beginning with
Champagnes and other fizz and
ending with beers and cider. Chile
looks good – as indeed it should –
alongside France, Spain and Italy.*

Virgin Wines

MAIL ORDER The Loft, St James' Mill,
Whitefriars, Norwich NR3 1TN
0870 164 9593 **FAX** (01603) 619277
CUSTOMER SERVICE 0870 164 9593
E-MAIL help@virginwines.com
WEBSITE www.virginwines.com
HOURS (office) Mon–Fri 8–7,
Sat–Sun 10–5, Internet 24 hrs
CARDS AmEx, MasterCard, Switch,
Visa **DISCOUNTS** regular special
offers **DELIVERY** £4.99 for UK,

N Ireland and Scottish Highlands, £6.99 for Saturday delivery within M25 **MINIMUM ORDER** 1 case. **G M**
✪ **Star attractions** *Internet retailer with hundreds of reasonably priced wines from all around the world. The list is organized by style rather than by grape variety, region or vintage and encourages the buyer to branch out and try new wines.*

Waitrose

HEAD OFFICE Doncastle Road, Southern Industrial Area, Bracknell, Berks RG12 8YA, **CUSTOMER SERVICE** 08456 049049, 166 licensed stores **E-MAIL** customerservice@waitrose. co.uk **WEBSITE** www.waitrose.com/wines **HOURS** Mon–Sat 8.30–7, 8 or 9, Sun 10–4 or 11–5 **CARDS** AmEx, Delta, MasterCard, Switch, Visa **DISCOUNTS** 5% for 6 bottles or more **DELIVERY** Home Delivery and Waitrose deliver for £3.95, Free for orders over £150 **EN PRIMEUR** Bordeaux, Port. **G T**

• **WAITROSE WINE DIRECT** order online at www.waitrose.com/winelist **E-MAIL** winedirect@waitrose.co.uk **DISCOUNTS** Vary monthly on featured cases **DELIVERY** Free for orders of £75 or more throughout UK mainland and Isle of Wight, otherwise £4.95 per delivery address.

✪ **Star attractions** *Still ahead of the other supermarkets in quality, value and imagination. Waitrose brings you the best from around the world. There are some very good clarets – such as the Côtes de Castillon Seigneurs d'Aiguilhe at £7.99 (see page 66) – and Burgundies, and some wonderful discoveries from southern France, the Rhône and the Loire. Italy, Germany, Australia and New Zealand have wines to suit every pocket. Despite its reputation for being a tad expensive, we found lots of really tasty stuff at under £5. All Waitrose wines are available from Waitrose Wine Direct.*

Waterloo Wine Co

OFFICE AND WAREHOUSE 6 Vine Yard, London SE1 1QL **SHOP** 59–61 Lant Street, London SE1 1QL (020) 7403 7967 **FAX** (020) 7357 6976 **E-MAIL** sales@waterloowine. co.uk **WEBSITE** www.waterloowine. co.uk **HOURS** Mon–Fri 10–6.30, Sat 10–5 **CARDS** AmEx, MasterCard, Switch, Visa **DELIVERY** Free 5 cases in central London (otherwise £5); elsewhere, 1 case £10, 2 cases £7.50 each. **G T**

✪ **Star attractions** *Quirky, personal list, strong in the Loire and making something of a speciality of the wines of the Waipara region of Canterbury, New Zealand. Waterloo are the UK agents for Minervois from Domaine La Tour Boisée – and this is one of the few places you'll find wines from Slovenia. Also a shortish but interesting list of clarets.*

Whitesides of Clitheroe

Shawbridge Street, Clitheroe, Lancs BB7 1NA (01200) 422281 **FAX** (01200) 427129 **E-MAIL** whitesides.wine@btconnect.com **HOURS** Mon–Fri 9–5.30, Sat 9–4 **CARDS** MasterCard, Switch, Visa **DISCOUNTS** 5% per case **DELIVERY** Free locally, elsewhere at cost. **G M T**

✪ **Star attractions** *A safe list of familiar names and flavours. I can find a reasonable number of wines I'd choose to drink here, especially from the New World, but also from Spain, Italy and Portugal.*

Wimbledon Wine Cellar

1 Gladstone Road, Wimbledon, London SW19 1QU (020) 8540 9979 **FAX** (020) 8540 9399
• 84 Chiswick High Road, London W4 1SY (020) 8994 7989 **FAX** (020) 8994 3683 **E-MAIL** enquiries@ wimbledonwinecellar.com or chiswick@wimbledon winecellar.com **WEBSITE** www.wimbledonwinecellar.com

HOURS (Wimbledon) Mon–Sat 10–9 (Chiswick) Mon–Sat 10–9, Sun 11–7 CARDS AmEx, MasterCard, Switch, Visa DISCOUNTS 10% off 1 case (with a few exceptions) DELIVERY Free local delivery. Courier charges elsewhere. EN PRIMEUR Burgundy, Bordeaux, Tuscany, Rhône.
C G M T
✪ **Star attractions** *Top names from Italy, Burgundy, Bordeaux, Rhône, Loire – and some of the best of the New World, especially Australia, South Africa and California. They don't issue a list, as stock changes so frequently, so you'll just have to go along to one of the shops and dig out your own treasure or look at their website.*

Wine & Beer World (Majestic)

HEAD OFFICE Majestic House, Otterspool Way, Watford, Herts WD25 8WW (01923) 298200 FAX (01923) 819105 PRE-ORDER (01923) 298297 • Rue du Judée, Zone Marcel Doret, Calais 62100, France (0033) 3 21 97 63 00 • Centre Commercial Carrefour, Quai L'Entrepôt, Cherbourg 50100, France (0033) 2 33 22 23 22 • Unit 3A, Zone La Française, Coquelles 62331, France (0033) 3 21 82 93 64 E-MAIL info@wineandbeer.co.uk WEBSITE www.wineandbeer.co.uk HOURS (Calais) 7 days 7–10 (Cherbourg) Mon–Sat 8.30–8 (Coquelles) 7 days 8–8. There is a free ferry crossing from Dover to Calais when your pre-order is over £300. All stores open bank holidays at the usual times CARDS MasterCard, Switch, Visa. **T**
✪ **Star attractions** *Savings of up to 50% on UK prices. The French arm of Majestic, handy for trips across the Channel: Calais is the largest branch, Coquelles the nearest to the Channel Tunnel terminal, while Cherbourg has a more limited range of wines. English-speaking staff.*

WATERLOO WINE CO

61 Lant Street London SE1 1QL Tel: 020 7403 7967

Email: sales@waterloowine.co.uk www.waterloowine.co.uk

Agents for independent producers from around the world, including Waipara West.

www.waiparawest.com

Winemark

3 Duncrue Place, Belfast BT3 9BU, 028 9074 6274 FAX 028 9075 1755; 71 branches E-MAIL info@ winemark.com WEBSITE www.winemark.com HOURS Branches vary, but in general Mon–Sat 10–10, Sun 12–8 CARDS Delta, MasterCard, Switch, Visa DISCOUNTS 5% on 6–11 bottles, 10% on 12 bottles or more. **G M T**
✪ **Star attractions** *Winemark is strong in the New World, with plenty of everyday drinking from the likes of Peter Lehmann in Australia, or you could trade up to Chateau Reynella or Hardys Eileen Shiraz at £49.99; also wines from New Zealand (Esk Valley, Villa Maria), California (Geyser Peak), Chile (Errázuriz Wild Ferment Chardonnay), and there's a shortish but good list of Bordeaux from older vintages.*

wine-pages-shop.com

Now, this sounds like a great idea, it's a website set up by wine writer Tom Cannavan, and offers mixed cases selected by Tom (with tasting notes to help you choose) and supplied direct from UK retailers. Tom has negotiated some exclusive discounts and persuaded the retailers to waive their delivery charges, so there are some truly amazing savings to be made.

Wine Rack

See Thresher Group.

The Wine Society

Gunnels Wood Road, Stevenage, Herts SG1 2BG (01438) 741177 FAX (01438) 761167 ORDER LINE (01438) 740222 E-MAIL memberservices@ thewinesociety.com WEBSITE www.thewinesociety.com HOURS Mon–Fri 8.30–9, Sat 9–5; showroom: Mon–Thurs 10–6, Fri 10–7, Sat 9.30–5.30 CARDS AmEx, MasterCard, Switch, Visa DISCOUNTS (per case) £3 per collection DELIVERY Free 1 case or more UK mainland and N Ireland. Collection facility at Montreuil, France, at French rates of duty and VAT EN PRIMEUR Bordeaux, Burgundy, Germany, Port, Rhône.

✪ **Star attractions** *The Wine Society has an inspired wine-buying team and this is an outstanding list. Bordeaux is excellent, with masses of well-chosen affordable wines as well as big names; Burgundy ditto; Rhône ditto; Loire, Italy, Spain, Portugal, all ditto, and lovely, classy New World wines. If you close your eyes and choose wines from this list with a pin, you'll always get something wonderful. The own label wines are as good as ever. You have to be a member to buy wine, but it costs only £40 for life and although it is necessary to be proposed by an existing member to join, the secretary of the society will propose you if you don't know any members.*

Wine Treasury

MAIL ORDER 69–71 Bondway, London SW8 1SQ (020) 7793 9999 FAX (020) 7793 8080 E-MAIL bottled@winetreasury.com WEBSITE www.winetreasury.com HOURS Mon–Fri 9.30–6.30 CARDS MasterCard, Switch, Visa DISCOUNTS 10% for unmixed dozens DELIVERY £10 per case, free 2 or more cases over £200, England and Wales; Scotland phone for more details MINIMUM ORDER 1 mixed case. M T

✪ **Star attractions** *California is a speciality here. There are the stunning Cabernet Sauvignons and Chardonnays from Stag's Leap Wine Cellars, Zinfandel from Cline Cellars, lots of tasty stuff from Joseph Phelps and much, much more. Italy looks just as good, with stars such as Sandrone and Roberto Voerzio from Piedmont, Tuscany's Castello di Ama and Sicily's Cusumano. But these top names don't come cheap.*

The Winery

4 Clifton Road, London W9 1SS (020) 7286 6475 FAX (020) 7286 2733 E-MAIL info@thewineryuk.com WEBSITE www.thewineryuk.com • The Winery at Liberty, Tudor Building , Second Floor, Liberty, Regent Street, London W1B 5AH (020) 7734 3239 E-MAIL liberty@thewineryuk.com HOURS Mon–Sat 11–9.30, Sun and public holidays 12–8 CARDS MasterCard, Switch, Visa DISCOUNTS 5% on a mixed case DELIVERY Free locally or for 3 cases or more, otherwise £10 per case. G M T

✪ **Star attractions** *Burgundy, Rhône, Italy and California are the specialities, and there's a range of grower Champagnes. The company sources its own wines, so it's a list to linger over – and a shop to linger in, especially when they're holding one of their regular tastings.*

Wines of Westhorpe

136a Doncaster Rd, Mexborough, South Yorks S64 0JW (01709) 584863 **FAX** (01709) 584863 **E-MAIL** wines@ westhorpe.co.uk **WEBSITE** www. westhorpe.co.uk **HOURS** Mon–Thu 9–9, Fri–Sat 9-6 **DISCOUNTS** Variable on 2 dozen or more **DELIVERY** Free UK mainland (except northern Scotland) **MINIMUM ORDER** 1 mixed case. **M** ✪ **Star attractions** *An excellent list for devotees of Eastern European wines – especially Hungarian and Romanian, as well as some from Chile, all at reasonable prices. From Hungary there's Kékfrankos, Kékoportó and Tokaji, as well as Szekszárdi Cabernet Franc and Budai Sauvignon Blanc.*

Wright Wine Co

The Old Smithy, Raikes Road, Skipton, N. Yorks BD23 1NP (01756) 700886 (01756) 794175 **FAX** (01756) 798580 **E-MAIL** bob@wineand whisky.co.uk **WEBSITE** www.wine andwhisky.co.uk **HOURS** Mon–Fri 9–6; Sat 10–5:30; open Sundays in December 10.30–4 **CARDS** MasterCard, Switch, Visa **DISCOUNTS** 10% unsplit case, 5% mixed case **DELIVERY** Free within 30 miles, elsewhere at cost. **G** ✪ **Star attractions** *South Africa, Australia and Alsace look good, but it's a pretty comprehensive list, so you'll also find short(ish) but well-chosen selections from Burgundy, the Loire, Portugal, Italy, Argentina – and everywhere else.*

Peter Wylie Fine Wines

Plymtree Manor, Plymtree, Cullompton, Devon EX15 2LE (01884) 277555 **FAX** (01884) 277557 **E-MAIL** peter@wylie-fine-wines. demon.co.uk **WEBSITE** www.wylie finewines.co.uk **HOURS** Mon–Fri 9–6 **CARDS** None **DISCOUNTS** Unsplit cases **DELIVERY** 1 case £20; 2 cases £11; 3–4 £6; 5 or more £4.50. **C M** ✪ **Star attractions** *Fascinating list of very old wines. Bordeaux from throughout the 20th century – there are umpteen 1961 clarets and a decent selection of serious wines from every vintage since. Red and white Bordeaux are the top performers on this list, but there are also a few Rhônes and Burgundies, plus ports going back to 1912, Madeiras to 1870.*

Yapp Brothers

The Old Brewery, Mere, Wilts BA12 6DY (01747) 860423 **FAX** (01747) 860929 **E-MAIL** sales@yapp.co.uk **WEBSITE** www.yapp.co.uk **HOURS** Mon–Sat 9–6 **CARDS** MasterCard, Switch, Visa **DISCOUNTS** £5 per case on collection **DELIVERY** £5 one case, 2 or more cases free. **C G M T** ✪ **Star attractions** *Rhône and Loire specialists who really know their way around these regions. They also have some of the hard-to-find wines of Provence (Bunan/Ch. de la Rouvière, Richeaume, Trévallon), Savoie and Corsica – oh, and two interlopers from Australia (Jasper Hill and Neagles Rock).*

Noel Young Wines

56 High Street, Trumpington, Cambridge CB2 2LS (01223) 844744 **FAX** (01223) 844736 **E-MAIL** admin@nywines.co.uk **WEBSITE** www.nywines.co.uk **HOURS** Mon–Sat 10–8, Sun 12–2 **CARDS** AmEx, MasterCard, Switch, Visa **DISCOUNTS** 5% for orders over £500 **DELIVERY** £7 first case, £4 subsequent cases, larger orders negotiable **EN PRIMEUR** Australia, Burgundy, Italy, Rhône. **G M T** ✪ **Star attractions** *Fantastic wines from just about everywhere. Think of a region and you'll find the best wines on Noel Young's list. Australia is a particular passion. There's a famously good Austrian list, some terrific Germans, plus beautiful Burgundies, Italians and dessert wines.*

Who's where

COUNTRYWIDE/MAIL ORDER ONLY
Aldi
Asda
L'Assemblage
Australian Wine Club
Bibendum Wine
Bordeaux Index
ChateauOnline
Co-op
Domaine Direct
High Breck Vintners
Justerini & Brooks
Laithwaites
Lay & Wheeler
Liberty Wines
O W Loeb
Majestic
Marks & Spencer
Mayfair Cellars
Montrachet
Morrisons
New Zealand Wines Direct
Oddbins
Oz Wines
Howard Ripley
Sainsbury's
Somerfield
Sunday Times Wine Club
Tesco
Thresher
The True Taste of Italy
Vin du Van
Vintage Roots
Virgin Wines
Waitrose
wine-pages-shop.com
Wine Rack
The Wine Society
Wine Treasury
Wines of Westhorpe
Peter Wylie Fine Wines

LONDON
John Armit Wines
Balls Brothers
H & H Bancroft Wines
Berkmann Wine Cellars
Berry Bros. & Rudd
Budgens
Cave Cru Classé
Corney & Barrow
Farr Vintners
Fortnum & Mason
Friarwood
Goedhuis & Co
Harvey Nichols
Haynes Hanson & Clark
Jeroboams

Lea & Sandeman
Moreno Wines
Philglas & Swiggot
Roberson
RSJ Wine Company
Unwins
Waterloo Wine Co
Wimbledon Wine Cellar
The Winery

SOUTH-EAST AND HOME COUNTIES
A&B Vintners
Bacchus Wine
Berry Bros. & Rudd
Budgens
Butlers Wine Cellar
Cape Wine and Food
Les Caves de Pyrene
Dodici
Flagship Wines
Le Fleming Wines
Flying Corkscrew
Hedley Wright
Maison du Vin
Turville Valley Wines
Unwins

WEST AND SOUTH-WEST
Averys Wine Merchants
Bennetts Fine Wines
Great Western Wine
Haynes Hanson & Clark
Hicks & Don
Laymont & Shaw
The Nobody Inn
Christopher Piper Wines
Reid Wines
Savage Selection
Stone, Vine & Sun
Yapp Brothers

EAST ANGLIA
Adnams
Amey's Wines
Anthony Byrne
Budgens
Corney & Barrow
Roger Harris Wines
Hicks & Don
Seckford Wines
T & W Wines
Unwins
Noel Young Wines

MIDLANDS
Bat & Bottle
Connolly's
Croque-en-Bouche
Gauntleys

S H Jones
Mills Whitcombe
Nickolls & Perks
Noble Rot Wine Warehouses
Portland Wine Co
Stevens Garnier
Tanners

WALES
Ballantynes
Devigne Wines
Irma Fingal-Rock
Moriarty Vintners
Terry Platt
Tanners

NORTH
Berkmann Wine Cellars
Booths
D Byrne
Great Northern Wine
Halifax Wine Co
Harvey Nichols
Martinez Wines
Nidderdale Fine Fines
Penistone Court Wine Cellars
Playford Ros
Richardson & Sons
Frank Stainton Wines
Vinceremos
Whitesides of Clitheroe
Wright Wine Co

SCOTLAND
Berkmann Wine Cellars
Cockburns of Leith
Corney & Barrow
Friarwood
Peter Green & Co
Harvey Nichols
Linlithgow Wines
Raeburn Fine Wines
Valvona & Crolla
Villeneuve Wines

NORTHERN IRELAND
Direct Wine Shipments
James Nicholson
Winemark

CHANNEL ISLANDS
Sommelier Wine Co

FRANCE
Millésima
Oddbins
Sainsbury's
Tesco Vin Plus
Wine & Beer World